TED

A Pawtobiography

My adventures on
GONE FISHING

PRAISE FOR
A PAWTOBIOGRAPHY

'I ate it in one sitting'

Dennis the Doberman

'I tore it up and used it as bedding'

Dora the cockapoo

'I buried it'

Luna the spaniel

*'I took it to the kennels on my holiday;
it helped a little to pass the time'*

Geoffrey the labrador

'What book?'

Bo the Briard

Pup Fiction

ALSO BY TED THE DOG
A Pawtobiography

TED

Pup Fiction

An epic journey with
GONE FISHING

TED THE DOG

(As told to Lisa Clark)

**EBURY
SPOTLIGHT**

Ebury Spotlight, an imprint of Ebury Publishing
UK | USA | Canada | Ireland | Australia
India | New Zealand | South Africa

Ebury Spotlight is part of the Penguin Random House group of companies whose
addresses can be found at global.penguinrandomhouse.com

Penguin Random House UK
One Embassy Gardens, 8 Viaduct Gardens, London SW11 7BW

penguin.co.uk
global.penguinrandomhouse.com

First published by Ebury Spotlight in 2025
1

Typeset by Clarkevanmeurs Design

Printed and bound in Great Britain by Clays Ltd, Elcograf S.p.A.

The authorised representative in the EEA is Penguin Random House Ireland, Morrison
Chambers, 32 Nassau Street, Dublin D02 YH68.

A CIP catalogue record for this book is available from the British Library

ISBN 9781529968439

Penguin Random House is committed to a sustainable future for our business, our readers
and our planet. This book is made from Forest Stewardship Council® certified paper.

To all my furry friends who are no longer here.
You'll never be forgotten.
Till we meet again. And we will.

CONTENTS

Part Deux: France

Prologue

I've had my briefcase for as long as I can remember. It was always very special to me. I think it's because it was all I ever really owned in the world. I'd been in four different homes before I was seven months old and it became like a security blanket for me.

Then I left it behind in the woods and someone else took it. It's remained my primary mission to get it back and who'd have thought that undertaking would lead me to foreign climes and a daring rescue mission, worthy of any blockbusting film.

Many people have asked me what's in the briefcase and why getting it back means so much to me.

Maybe the answer lies with the film supremo Quentin Tarantino, who said the value of the briefcase in his classic 1994 movie *Pulp Fiction* lay not in its contents but in the briefcase itself.

You could draw that analogy with fishing as well. It's not always about the fish you catch but the joy of fishing itself. Being on the riverbank with Paul and Bob is one of the greatest pleasures in my life, alongside food and most recently my passion for parkour.

All these delights are about to collide in one big European adventure and you are most welcome to join me on the ride.

Do you know what they call a Quarter Pounder with cheese in France?

I was about to find out.

PART ONE
HOME TURF

CHAPTER ONE

How It All Began

If you read my last book you'll know that ... what, you didn't read it? Why on earth not? Everyone else did. Where were you and what's your excuse?

There's still time, so go and get one, I'll wait for you. Hurry up and don't even think about looking in the bargain bins. It was an instant classic. It's probably at the British Library by now. I hear paw-signed copies are changing hands on the black market for vast sums and large bones.

While we wait for those misfits to get their copy of my *Pawtobiography*, I'll briefly summarise what it was all about, in case those of you who read it haven't committed every word to memory.

I was born into a litter of six puppies in 2012. They didn't like me and I didn't care for them either. My mother was at best indifferent and I never knew my father. Nor, as it turned out, did my mother.

I was the last puppy to be sold, just before Christmas, at a drastically reduced price. As I recall, I think it was for a family pack of iced mince pies. The writing was

4

clearly on the wall. I mean, who buys the iced version of mince pies?

They didn't really take to me in my first home, even though I was a surprise present, supposedly fulfilling two young boys' ultimate dream of finally owning their own dog. They soon got bored of me and went back to their pet PlayStations instead.

I was dumped, alongside the wilting Christmas tree, after the festive celebrations were over. I was only six months old and it wasn't really the best start in life or the outcome I'd dreamt of.

All I had was my beloved leather briefcase, which I subsequently and stupidly left behind in the woods where I used to play games with the squirrels.

The family deposited me, all alone, outside a dogs' home and went on their merry way. To where, I simply don't know but of course I wished them all the very best for the future.

I spent six months incarcerated, which, far from breaking me, gave me skills and confidence way beyond my years.

I made lifelong friends in the home and came tantalisingly close to reuniting with my briefcase, as one of the other inmates, a rough pitbull called Vinnie, had found it and was holding it ransom.

When I was finally adopted into my forever home, I was forced to leave my briefcase behind, which was pretty devastating, but as you'll know only too well, I am made of tougher stuff and that's when I vowed I'd stop at nothing to get it back.

In my lovely new home, I met my soulmate, and the mother I never had, a beautiful pedigree Old English sheepdog called Dolly. We instantly bonded and although we could not have been more different, we adored each other. She was everything I wasn't. Poised, dainty and fragrant.

I muscled my way onto *Gone Fishing* with Bob Mortimer and Paul Whitehouse in 2017 and quickly turned a pretty successful television show into a beloved national institution.

Dolly died when she was almost 14. That did break me, I'll be honest.

I decided to write my first book for several reasons. To honour the legacy of Dolly and to teach you human muppets how to properly look after your pets, because some of you are severely lacking in the basics and need quite a bit of training yourselves.

I decided to write this second book for one main reason: You lot still have a hell of a lot to learn.

So settle down and prepare yourself for more revelations, showbiz secrets and a few laughs at Bob and Paul's expense along the way. When did I ever let you down?

My dearly departed friend Dolly was my inspiration to write, alongside a steady supply of pocket meat.

CHAPTER TWO

The Life of an Author

My first book, *A Pawtobiography*, was published in November 2024 and rocked the book world off its very axis.

I don't want to wag my own tail, but the fact is I outsold many of my heroes, like Al Pacino, Cher and David Jason.

And I shifted more copies than Rick Astley.

The whole journey, from being an unwanted skinny runt to a star of the small screen and then a bestselling dog author, was a hoot.

I didn't read the reviews of my book. I'm happy for you to keep your opinions to yourself but I did chuckle at this comment in the *Sunday Times*:

'We've had plenty of books about animals in the bestseller lists this year, but this week, unusually, features a book by an animal – Ted the Patterdale terrier from *Gone Fishing*, to be precise. And if he had sold just 101 more copies, Ted would have beaten "Big Dog" Boris Johnson.'

Make of that what you will.

Where is Boris now? Licking his wounds – and not for the first time either.

It's odd, the selection of people you rub paws with on the publishing publicity circuit. Little Bob was out and about, shuffling around with his *Hotel Avocado* book, Jeremy Clarkson was banging on about farming, Miranda Hart was admitting telling porkies and so, of course, was Boris. Again.

I ended up being number two in the bestseller chart at Christmas, just sniffing up Miranda's backside, which actually was quite pleasant. Much sweeter than Paul or Bob's anyway.

So, does that make me a famous dog? And even if it did, would that make any difference?

Sure, I get recognised these days. I don't really mind but it can be quite awkward when I'm in the middle of a major clear-out in the park of a morning. It's not the ideal time for a selfie or a pawtograph. Let's just say the most eager fans get a little more than they bargained for when they bend down to greet me – a right noseful, in fact.

Has it changed me? You can judge for yourself in this book.

Spoiler alert: No.

I did get quite a bunch of fan mail, with plenty of offers to boot.

Aslan wrote to me from the dental practice where he works in Turkey, offering me some new veneers.

Sifting through my fan mail;
the good, the bad and the rather saucy.

Edgar wrote from a clinic in Latvia offering me free weight-loss injections.

I declined both, not because I was insulted by their offers, far from it, but because I wouldn't have the first clue how to get there. Otherwise I would have been bang up for a bit of a glow up.

I know I have 'unusual' looks but that's what makes me stand out from the crowd. I only get miffed when people openly laugh or point at me and ask if I'm related to Rylan. His teeth are not natural, I'll leave it there.

I also had plenty of female admirers who sent me pictures, some of which I can only describe as somewhat on the fruity side. I expect you think I put the raciest ones in the bin – well, I didn't because they can't be recycled, so I have kept them safe in a basket by my bedside and every now and again I have a quick look through them to check they're all still in order.

I will admit to being slightly miffed that with all those millions of readers, no one managed to find my bloody briefcase. Did you even bother to look?

Honestly, if you want a job doing properly, you have to do it yourself, as you'll find out.

I'm getting on a bit now and I should be able to spend more time relaxing in bed. To be honest, I do spend 80% of my time asleep but the other 25% it's all go go go.

I made it clear in my last book, maths is not my strong point and it has not improved.

You may well be wondering how my life *has* improved and I'd be more than happy to tell you. You paid for this book – it's the least you deserve.

Bob has, on occasion, allowed me to sit up front in his car, demoting Paul to the mosh pit in the back. It's a whole new ball game at the business end of his motor, there are heated seats and everything. The coffee cup holders are full to the brim of … actually I'm not sure what's in there all told, but I do like to dip my paw in to have a taste. It's like a lucky dip.

I also get to play around with the audio system, although that does really annoy Bob. He tends to listen to old bloke music like Free and Bad Company, which they certainly are on our long journeys.

I prefer a bit of drum and bass, like Chase & Status at max vol, but Bob just complains and says they don't make records like they used to. Thank you, Captain Obvious – times change, mate, get with it.

As you can tell I'm still as charming and gracious as I always was. And I'm pulling no punches in this book.

Enjoy. And if for whatever reason you didn't pay for this, I expressly forbid you to read on.

CHAPTER THREE

After Dolly

I'll tell you first a little about my day trip to the Museum of Naval Firepower in Gosport, which was a gift to try and cheer me up after I lost my dear friend Dolly, and it was a good effort, to be fair.

I was thrilled to learn it is also known locally as the Explosion Factory.

You can marvel at missiles, torpedoes, small arms, cannons and guns, as well as the ammunition that was used inside them. To be fair, that takes all of about 15 minutes and I couldn't really be arsed to read all the historical literature about dates and all that guff, you know, the boring bits you just want to gloss over, but there was a nice café looking over the harbour so when I'd had my fill of weaponry, I checked that out.

I managed to hoover up plenty of discarded pasties, once I'd scared off the mouthy, greedy gulls who were lurking menacingly by the rubbish. Is there an unwritten rule for humans that you should leave your waste in the vicinity of a bin, or around a bin, but never actually in the bin itself?

Despite that, it was a fairly pleasant day trip. My over-all review, however, must highlight the lack of actual live explosions, so I can only give it one star. Don't @ me.

Museums remind me of the time Bob asked Paul how short a time it was acceptable to look at a painting in an art gallery, before it was deemed suitable to move on. I've often thought the same about other dogs' bums.

There's an unwritten rule in our community which says you may inhale from a stranger's jacksie for no less than 10 seconds and no more than 30. And after the initial maximum 30 seconds has elapsed, it is NOT polite to chase after them for one extra bite of the arse cherry. Just so you know and remember not to pull your dog away from the other dog (or sniffee) until after the requisite time has passed.

If you are lucky enough to have a dog sniff your crotch, that is known as a sign of affection, which makes sense if you think about it. But I wouldn't think about it for too long.

Dogs sniffing bums is our equivalent of shaking hands – especially if you've not washed your hands recently. It's a dog's way of communicating. One good sniff of a back-side can determine if we have ever met before and if we are to be friends or enemies.

Each dog's odour is entirely unique to them. I s'pose it's a bit like your breath. Only ours comes out the other end and doesn't smell of stale garlic.

You'll have already noted (or at least you should have done if you are paying attention and not arsing around on your phone at the same time as reading – yes, I've seen you do that), this book is not just a rip-roaring, swashbuckling adventure, it's sprinkled with top tips as to how you can understand and ultimately treat your own dogs better.

Obviously, I have insider knowledge on a dog's world, how our minds work and how we really feel about you guys, therefore I can guarantee that much of what you read in this book will make a lasting impression on you.

All that for under 20 quid.

And there is no money-back guarantee if you're not entirely satisfied, just to be clear.

I'm not recounting the details of losing Dolly again simply because I can't. You'll know if you've lost a best friend, furry or human, how painful it can be. It leaves a massive void in your life and, for me, one of the hardest things is that the world keeps on turning. Everybody else's life is the same, apart from yours. It can leave you feeling so lonely and desolate.

I remember going to the park not long after Dolly had gone and watching all these dogs happily playing with their balls or running around pointlessly chasing each other without a care in the world ... whereas I felt a massive lump in my heart and my paws were like lead.

They say grief is the price we pay for love …
and I felt bankrupt.

Dolly's ashes were brought home, in a lovely little wooden box with her name engraved on a brass plaque. I couldn't bear to look at it at first. Her collar and name tag were left in my bed. They smelt so strongly of her familiar floral fragrance and I slept with them every night.

The loss of a companion instantly changes all our routines. It's the same for us dogs as it is for you humans. The silence when you come home, the void in the bed next to you, the food bowls standing empty and so many pockets full of unused poo bags.

I know they say 'grief is the price of love' but that only makes me wonder, if I'd loved Dolly half as much as I did, would she have lived half a bit longer?

CHAPTER FOUR

Home Alone

Alone in my room, I discovered the 'dog web', which is very much like the dark web, but for dogs only. I lost countless hours falling down the scroll hole. I think it's also known as going down a rabbit hole, which I'd had plenty of practice doing, and it wasn't an altogether unpleasant experience.

There were so many forums debating all manner of dog-related issues.

Dog's Net was always especially busy and, deary me, did it descend into complete savagery and bitchiness in the blink of an eye. It was almost as bad as Dog Next Door, where dogs would endlessly debate the most mundane and pointless topics.

'Has anyone noticed how muddy the park has become? Can't they stop the incessant rain?'

'The dog poo bin was full today. What do we pay our council taxes for?'

'I saw Cherry out once again without a coat. That poor animal must be so cold. Shall we start a GoFundMe?'

Doom scrolling never ends well, but it can be fun.

A word about coats: they suit some dogs and not others. A bit like you lot with hats. There are some people who just shouldn't wear hats, simple as. Bob is an exception, not a rule.

Personally, I hate coats. They restrict my movement and make me feel like an old git. If I have been made to suffer a coat, I simply do not move, not a muscle. Eventually it will get taken off and then and only then will I agree to proceed with my walk.

There are some breeds who benefit from an extra layer: thin jobs like greyhounds or whippets; ones that tend to soak up water like a sponge, that's your spaniels; and those with pointless little legs like a dachshund or corgi.

How about those onesies for dogs? Good grief. I'm sorry but they look completely ridiculous. I know they are supposed to stop your dog from getting muddy but that's a little bit like buying a pair of shoes and never wearing them out in case they get dirty. I swear when I see a poor pooch squeezed mercilessly into his onesie, they raise their eyes to the heavens as I walk past.

There's even a dry robe for dogs on the market. Have you not read what they say about people who wear dry robes as an everyday coat? It doesn't make light reading. It's fine, of course, if you are intending to swim the Channel, which I suspect none of us are.

I was doom scrolling to specifically look for a way to get over my grief but ended up learning how to open tins of dog food with only one paw and how to silently remove the squeak from inside toys without leaving any trace of your handiwork.

There were some brilliant viral reels on there as well. I spent hours and hours watching various dogs bumscooting down hills and some really funny compilations of dogs trying to leap up onto kitchen counters and failing miserably, crashing to the ground in a heap.

My favourite was a reel of dogs nicking stuff from their owners and hiding it. They were masters at it. Keys, socks, phones, pants, hair ties, scarves and shoes. They then put them up for sale. I guess it's a way to make a living. I was shocked to discover a pair of Armani pants went for a tenner – used pants? Really? And yes, I did buy them. Dead soft they are too. I sometimes use them as pyjamas when we're away.

I immediately stopped this addictive habit when I came across a rather tasteless grooming site. It was slo-mo shots of various dogs being bathed, washed and clipped. It was something that once you have watched, you can't unsee. Those poor dogs, forced to look pretty and smell sweet just for their owners' benefit.

Have you seen the shots of dogs that have been dyed all sorts of different colours? They're made to look like different animals, like a tiger and that. For crying out loud, pack that in. We are not toys. We are highly intelligent, sensitive animals with real feelings and emotions.

If you want to play dress up, go get yourself a My Little bloody Pony and leave us well out of it.

I'm well aware that smart phones are not the answer to relieving boredom. Anyway, I don't actually own a phone, I just borrow any that I can find. No, I don't steal them, they are purely on a short-term loan.

I think there should be one day a week when phones are banned completely. Can you imagine how different all our lives would be, without constant interruption or distraction? People would actually look at each other and maybe even talk to each other face to face – go with me on this – we'd have to get back to reading maps and shopping in real stores and reading books (this is not a sales pitch) and looking at photos in real albums. Think about how our whole world would change in an instant in just one day.

Be rather dull, wouldn't it – let's scrap that thought and never speak of it again.

CHAPTER FIVE

Gone Fishing

This social isolation was getting me nowhere. It was just making me a crosspatch. I didn't even want to go fishing.

Yes, dogs can suffer from depression and it's not pleasant.

Fishing is now prescribed by the National Health Service to help humans who are struggling, to get them out into the fresh air and amongst nature, but even though I knew it would help me, I simply couldn't motivate myself this time.

Paul and Bob went to Ireland and they mentioned on the show that I couldn't join them because of my reputation. That is partly true but mostly it was because I didn't want to go and have any fun – and I knew the worst thing about it would be coming home again to an empty nest, with no Dolly dog to greet me, asking me to tell her all about the trip.

Paul and Bob tried everything to persuade me to join them. Bob said he had a batch of fresh Spam and Paul said he would let me get snout deep into the bait bucket whenever I wanted. When I still refused, Paul added that I could tread all over his rod if that would help, but there was no persuading me this time.

I spent a lot of time moping in my bed.

Full disclosure, I have a lot of beds. Ted's beds baby, Ted's beds.

Five, to be precise. A blue one, a wicker basket, a fluffy one, a harder one and one that looks like a furry doughnut, which is a favourite as I can sink deep into it, shut the outside world out and not look at anyone or anything.

Oh, and I have outdoor beds as well. And a hammock. And a deck chair.

A heated bed is on my birthday list. Must ascertain when my birthday actually is.

I still couldn't really get to sleep wherever I tried. I was restless and twitchy and couldn't get comfortable. When I did manage to drop off, I dreamt about Dolly.

During REM sleep, the brain activity of dogs is very similar to that of humans, so we too play back experiences and memories in our dreams.

I dreamt mostly about chasing foxes and cats and whacking them over the head with my briefcase but Dolly was always wafting around in the background, giving me the look that said, 'Violence is never the answer, Edward. You know better than that.'

My dreams left me somewhat exhausted.

I was dreading her birthday, which would really mark her loss. But I don't know the actual date she was born so that was a little pointless.

I admit I was swimming in self-pity, and it was only getting worse. My general grump wasn't helped by the fact I was doing Dry January. This meant I was only willing to go on a walk if it was dry. January is such a long, wet month, so I hardly set foot outside.

I decided to contact Bob. Both Paul and Bob have often talked on *Gone Fishing* about reaching out to friends if you're feeling down and trying to express your emotions, so I knew he'd understand.

Our semi-resident doctor, Dr Anand Patel has also told us countless times not to bottle things up and to talk to people before our feelings spiral out of control. I knew he was right but men in particular have issues discussing their personal emotions and I was no different.

I tentatively picked up the nearest phone and texted Bob:

Ted: Alright. How was Ireland?

Bob: I had a tricky moment with Paul when he insists I lost a salmon of a lifetime but it wasn't my fault.

Ted: You sure?

Bob: No.

Ted: Would it have helped if I was there?

Bob: No.

Ted: Not sure I'll come fishing again.

Bob: Why not?

Ted: Wanna stay in bed.

Bob: You'll get fat – ter.

Ted: You ain't exactly a waif, mate.

Bob: Just pull your scruffy self together and come fishing. You can't live in the past.

Ted: Can if I want to.

Bob: Shall I get you another dog?

Ted: No. I want a cat.

Bob: You wouldn't get on with a cat.

Ted: I know, that's the point.

Bob: What if I told you Tony Blackburn is coming on the next shoot and is going to DJ at a special party for us?

Ted: Now you're talking. Where do I need to be?

And so I gave myself a good shake, reluctantly had a swift bath, cleaning only the key areas, and dragged my sorry arse out again.

CHAPTER SIX

Getting Back in the Saddle

I must admit it was good to see the old fishing gang. They hadn't changed. They still smelt the same – a heady mix of rubbery waders, stale fish and beer. And that was just Paul and Bob.

I did expect a little more of a fanfare on my return. Some bunting or a banner saying 'All hail, the king has returned' or a massive welcome-home cake and champagne, but all I got was a few pats and some stale pocket meat. Mind you, Bob's pocket meat is always stale, because it lives in his stale pocket.

Nothing much had changed with the *Gone Fishing* crew, which was rather comforting. There was still the ritual faff of getting going in the morning and the plaintiff cries of 'I need coffee', 'more coffee', 'hotter coffee', 'sweeter coffee', 'bigger coffee', 'another coffee'.

What is it with you lot and coffee? You can't go more than one quick trot down any high street without being assaulted by a tsunami of coffee shops. You think you're being amusing with the names of these shops but frankly they are not funny at all.

Thanks a Latte. The Daily Grind. Déjà Brew.

Childish.

Why not tell it like it is and call it *Overpriced Addiction*?

Don't think I haven't noticed how you are trying to lure us dogs into your caffeine cult by tempting us with so-called Pup Cups, Puppuccinos and possibly the worst name of them all, Cappawccinos. Keep your sad addictions to yourself please.

We don't need coffee, we don't need booze and we don't need fags. You go ahead and knacker yourselves if you want to. Leave us canines well out of it.

I was still feeling a touch grouchy, have you noticed?

Turns out, the place we were staying at for this trip was pretty damn cool and my mood slowly began to lift. It was called 616 Venue and was in the heart of Sherwood Forest in Nottinghamshire. It was also known as the party house and it didn't disappoint on that front.

We were all staying there for the duration of the shoot, with a room each. We were like frisky rabbits in our own little warrens. This was somewhat unusual because normally Bob, Paul and I are kept separate from the crew, for our own safety. But here there was no such segregation. We were all stuck together.

The stars of the show often get to stay in slightly posher accommodation because we don't make as much mess. I didn't really mind but I always knew where the real party was at – with the crew.

Paul and Bob tended to slope off at an early hour to get their beauty sleep. Maybe they need to go to bed even earlier for that to begin to have some effect.

Dogs need beauty sleep as well. That's probably why I look as good as I do.

One of the most memorable – and cold – places we ever stayed was St Nicholas' Church, near Epping Forest. I gather it's called 'champing', which unsurprisingly means camping out in a church, and I really wouldn't recommend it as a new hobby. It was freezing cold. Paul and I had our own sleeping bags and Bob squeezed himself into a sleep suit, which looked like something he'd borrowed from NASA.

At this point I would like to address a rumour which has been swirling around since that episode aired. It was brought to my attention that many members of the public did not believe we all stayed in the church overnight. The keyboard warriors determined that we slipped off, once the crew had left, and stayed in a local hostelry.

I wish.

Like much of what you tend to lap up on the internet, this is entirely false.

I tell you, we all slept there. I say 'slept', which works if one hour of shut-eye counts, and I did say in no uncertain terms to the boys in the morning that I would NOT be doing that again. They didn't put up much of a fight.

Back at the 616, which was a darn sight more appealing than the church, I noticed there were some domestic ducks hanging out in the courtyard. They were aptly called runner ducks and they all looked like they were in a right hurry to get somewhere. Normally I would give them a bit of a chase but as I was a VIP guest in this place, I decided to behave, at least while people were watching me.

I once had a very near miss with a duck which could have landed me in a lot of bother. We were fishing on a private lake in Norfolk and there was this cute little duck sitting (do ducks sit or do they squat?). Either way it was sat very peacefully, looking over the lake. I decided to play my version of chicken and give it a bit of a fright and ran at it full pelt. My version of full pelt, which is still pretty fast, thank you.

It didn't move. It just sat there. I found it impossible to stop in time and bashed it straight into the lake. There was even a feather or two stuck in my teeth. Incidentally, they work very well as floss.

I later found out that this duck was matey with another dog who lived on the estate, so he saw no reason to move when I went for him. Could have been pretty awks if I'd squished it.

I shouted across the lake, 'Sorry, mate, was just playing a game of chicken. You were supposed to move out the way!'

She ruffled and wagged her tail feathers and stared hard at me before saying, 'Your teeth are so bad you could eat an apple through a fence.'

What an impudent duck. Next time I'll get more than just a few back feathers out of her.

The evening of my first shoot back, I still felt a little out of sorts, so Bob allowed me to sleep in his room, even though I had been allocated one of my own. I did let him choose the side of the bed he wanted to sleep on. Selfless, I know.

Over half of dog owners sleep with their pets, and in case you're thinking of all the mud, fleas and dirt left on your silky sheets, let me tell you sleeping with your BFF has been proven to increase your flow of oxytocin, thus reducing your stress levels, even though it will increase your washing loads. So stop being selfish and share your bed. And don't scrimp on splitting the pillows either.

I asked Bob to read to me in bed. I know that could be seen as somewhat needy but a) I don't care and b) I needed some comfort. I was hoping for something racy like *A Clockwork Orange* or *The Wasp Factory* but then I saw a copy of his autobiography *And Away …* and pointed to that.

I knew he'd like that. I'm no shmuck. I know which side my biscuits are baked.

Let's see the cut of his jib, I thought. Not many people can write a bestselling autobiography and I did wonder how this little muppet had managed it.

Bobby's beautiful bedtime stories.

He started to read:

'I am fifty-six years old. My life is trundling along like a podgy golden retriever being dragged along the pavement ...'

I checked to see if he was reading my book or his book.

'I sleep on a thick memory foam mattress so there's always a certain stickiness to my rising.'

It must be my book.

'I look in the mirror and see before me a face like a puddle of spaghetti hoops, bloated, creased and tired.'

No, this was definitely his book.

He continued, 'I am about to embark on a month-long tour with my comedy partner Jim Moir ...'

I heard no more as I drifted off into a deep sleep – all four paws firmly sprawled all over the wrong side of the bed.

I couldn't resist giving Bob's head a quick lick in the night. I wanted to see what it tasted like. I'll tell you at the end of the book. It was quite unexpected.

CHAPTER SEVEN

The Legendary Tony Blackburn

Bob told me Tony Blackburn was to be a special surprise guest for Paul on this shoot. I know Tony is a regular on Radio 2 with his show *Sounds of the 60s*. It's not really my kind of thing; I'm more into Romesh Ranganathan's *For the Love of Hip Hop* but I could see how Tony would be a thrill for Paul and of course our viewers.

Not really, I couldn't see that at all, but Bob assured me he would be.

While Paul was getting ready for the evening, Bob and I were joined by Tony in the basement bar. Tony was talking about how he used to work on the pirate ships – I could hardly believe my little ears, what a guy. I gathered what he was doing back then was highly illegal. I imagined barrels of confiscated rum and all sorts of hardcore activity.

Pirate comes from the Greek word 'peirates' – one who attacks – which made Tony immediately shoot up in my estimation. He didn't look exactly fierce but maybe he was quite the thing back in the day.

Paul was totally surprised and utterly delighted when he saw Tony was there. They hugged like long-lost pals and then started this odd ritual of speaking in a strange way and repeating 'great mate' and 'poptastic' over and again. I presumed these were piracy phrases – to think I never knew Paul was once a pirate as well.

It made me wonder what Bob had been before he was an expert fisherman. I knew he'd had some kind of army training but he had never been more specific. Maybe given how accomplished he was in and around the water, he'd been part of the SBS, the UK's elite maritime special forces. He had the look of a salty old sea dog.

The night really kicked off when Paul and Tony took to the decks as 'Smashy & Nicey' and started spinning the party tunes. I gather it was all for charity or something. The pair of them were in their element. It was rather a magical scene to witness.

The whole crew took to the floor. I never knew Bob was such an elite dancer. He can really bust some moves. He was like a cross between Fred Astaire and Shaggy. That's Shaggy from *Scooby-Doo*, not the one who sang about banging about on various floors of an apartment in New York.

Who knew people this old could be so much fun?

I slunk off about midnight, along with the other golden oldies, leaving the crew to make their own mischief. I was hoping to catch the ducks by surprise but sadly they were locked away.

I drifted off to sleep quickly but I did have the rather infuriating tune 'You Ain't Seen Nothin' Yet' whirling round and round in my head.

CHAPTER EIGHT

Dognapped

The trip to the River Trent was a great success. Both Bob and Paul caught a 'good fish', which only made me wonder what a really bad fish looked like. They all looked the same to me. Pretty irritated at being caught.

Arriving back home again, I felt exactly as I had expected and dreaded: empty.

I thought maybe, just maybe, they had decided to get another dog, hopefully a Patterdale I could train up and get into trouble with, but all I still had was Dolly's collar for company.

I have been told dogs come into our lives to teach us about love and they depart to teach us about loss. What if I didn't give a toss about loss?

Paul and Bob didn't have to ask if I was up for the next trip. I didn't unpack from the last one. I was instantly ready to go and I didn't even bother to wash this time.

I guess I had let myself go a little – I could even smell me from a distance and it wasn't particularly pleasant. I didn't think anyone would even notice, much less care.

Dogs sweat through their paws, and bearing in mind the number of germs picked up on a daily basis on those sticky little pads, mix them with plenty of moisture and you have one heady smell to contend with. Soz.

In America it's charmingly known as 'Frito feet' so the equivalent over here would be 'Wotsit feet', which I'm sure would delight Bob.

We were going to the most northerly chalk stream in the UK, Driffield Beck in East Yorkshire.

Whoop de whoop – alert the media and stop all the clocks. They all look the same to me. Some have more complex smells but once you've rolled on one riverbank, you've rolled on them all.

As soon as we got there, I lost no time searching for the murkiest bit of the riverbank and fully indulged myself, really rubbing the dirt in deep. I had a good base layer already and this fresh topping was just the tonic.

Bob and Paul were not impressed. Bob asked, 'What would your parents say if they saw you in this state?'

What parents? Mum wasn't bothered about me right from the off and I never knew my father. And thanks for bringing that up, by the way.

I found some more fresh muck to marinate in and I noticed that Paul and Bob kept their distance from me. They didn't invite me to sleep over with them that evening. Their loss.

On the morning of the second day, Bob told Paul to carry on fishing as he was taking me somewhere special. He's such a legend. I wondered if it would be a dog park (as long as it was better than that awful soggy place we once went to in Scotland) or maybe a pet shop where I could glare at some rabbits and kittens, or maybe even a firework factory?

We pulled up outside a place called Wagtails. Name seems promising, I thought. Sounds like a happy place.

As I got out of the car, an all too familiar smell suddenly hit me right between the eyes. It was a clean, fruity smell. The little sod had only taken me to a dog groomer.

I tried to escape, but canny Bob was holding tight to my lead. I felt sure this was false imprisonment or kidnapping, something along those lines.

Once I was dragged inside, a lovely lady called Louisa took one sniff of me and declared a code red. She called for reinforcements and put a double apron on. Talk about making an unnecessary fuss.

They manhandled me into the bathtub and secured me so I couldn't escape. I'd given in to my fate at this stage anyway. I realised resistance was futile as I was heavily outnumbered.

I was washed all over with the canine equivalent of Matey bubble bath, then they gave me a warm mud treatment, which sadly they rinsed off before finishing me off

I'll get you back for this, Bob!

with a blueberry facial. The sticky mixture was applied all around my muzzle and I could taste the soapy blueberries all over my tongue.

Just when I thought it was finally over, I was blown dry, which was highly superfluous, and then – I can hardly bring myself to say these words – I was presented with a small, red velvet bow, which was ceremoniously attached to my collar. I couldn't bear to look at it.

I have never been so humiliated (or clean) in my whole life.

I smelt like a bloody fruit smoothie.

To be fair, the mud bath did feel good and soothed my joints but I couldn't get the stink of blueberries out of my 'tache for days.

Bob picked me up a few hours later, although it felt like days had passed by then.

'Oh Teddy, is that really you?' he asked when he clapped eyes on the new squeaky-clean me.

Of course it is, you muppet. You dumped me here, I thought.

As soon as my paws set foot on the riverbank, I headed straight for a muddy puddle and rolled around until most of the fruity smell had at least begun to loosen and the bow was now obsolete.

Paul and Bob were both rather cross and said, 'That's the last time we bother to get you clean.'

Mission accomplished. That'll teach them to trick me.

CHAPTER NINE

The Thing in the Cage

This time, when I got back home, I could instantly see a big cage had been plonked in the corner of the kitchen.

Had they found the secret stash under my bed? Or had they been reading my text messages? Whatever I'd done, I didn't think I deserved to be locked up. Of course, I can pick locks in minutes, but this was the last thing I expected to have to do in my own home.

I slunk upstairs before anyone saw me.

I couldn't sleep that night for worrying. What on earth had I done wrong? Why couldn't they just talk to me about it? I wondered how long I'd be locked up for. Days, weeks?

Surely not. I wondered if I could remove the cage with my teeth and lob it into the back garden. Perhaps not, it looked pretty sturdy. There would be collateral damage. To my teeth.

In the morning, I went straight downstairs, and to my horror, there was now a creature asleep in the cage. What was it that had to be kept under lock and key?

It looked like a baby tiger. This could actually be fun, I thought.

I poked my nose through the bars and took a big deep sniff. It smelt like a baby. It clearly was a tiger cub. Result! We could make one heck of a security team together.

It was no fun while it was asleep, so I found a fork on the kitchen floor and poked it sharply in the ribs a couple of times.

Oh God, did it then howl.

I thought I'd get into trouble for waking it up so I tried to soothe it by running my teeth along the bars of the cage to make a sweet lullaby but this only made it cry even more.

I ran upstairs and got Dolly's favourite toy, the little sheep, and rammed it through the bars. This did the trick and it stopped whingeing.

Then it proceeded to rip the toy to shreds, tearing it from limb to limb. I watched, horrified, as all the stuffing cascaded out of its little woolly body and onto the floor of the cage.

The sheep was massacred. There was nothing left but a shell and a tuft of fluff on its head – which was now detached from its body.

I showed the thing in the cage my teeth. It laughed.

I'd had quite enough of this. It came into my house uninvited, ate the one thing Dolly left me and had absolutely no respect for who I was.

The alien has landed.

I stomped upstairs back to bed. An hour or so later it was crying again. I was at the end of my tether and stomped back downstairs to confront it.

As I approached the cage, it said, 'I'm sorry I destroyed your sheep.'

'Apology unaccepted,' I replied. 'What kind of a monster are you?'

In a heavy French accent, it said, 'I am a Briard. A lady Briard.'

She was no lady. She was a psychopath.

I wondered what a Briard was when it was at home, particularly as it was now in MY home.

A quick search on the net revealed what it was:

*The **Briard** or Berger de Brie is a French breed of large shepherd dog, traditionally used for herding sheep and to defend them.*

This one was clearly a mutant. Far from guarding my sheep, it ate it.

Anyway, why did we need a bloody shepherd dog? I mean, I am a ratter, so I have a place at the table, know what I mean?

'Are you staying long?' I asked, dreading the reply.

'Je ne sais pas,' it replied.

'What is your name?' I continued.

'Je ne sais pas,' it said again.

I'm NOT saying I felt sorry for it but clearly it had no idea where it was or what it was doing here. Maybe it had been dropped off by mistake? I know how unreliable some delivery companies can be, often taking stuff to the wrong address.

I decided to let it out of the cage. Maybe it needed to do some herding or something?

It crept out. It was an odd-looking thing, like a furry slug.

It whizzed around the kitchen and then peed on the carpet. No manners whatsoever.

It then tried to climb on my back and bite my stump. I shook it off but then it went for my paws ... and my ears were next. It was chasing me round and round the kitchen island.

I felt like a contestant being royally pasted on *Gladiators*. She didn't have a pugil stick but she didn't need one. Her paws were like massive shovels.

I'd had my fill of this foreign intruder and I was in no mood to engage with it any longer. I couldn't beat it and I certainly wasn't going to join it. I had to leave. But where the hell could I go? I had a horrible feeling of déjà vu. Don't exactly know what that means, but I knew I had to get out.

I went upstairs, grabbed Dolly's collar and left.

CHAPTER TEN

Banged Up Again

I decided to go back to the dogs' home I'd come from and speak to my old mates about this imposter. Maybe it had even come from there in the first place? I knew the vague direction to go in and I followed my trusty nose.

Our noses are as unique as your fingerprints. Bet you weren't taught that at school.

It felt good to be back on the road again. Just me. No muppets. No screaming slug. I had quite a spring in my step, which I don't take for granted these days.

I spent the first night in the woods, which felt oddly reassuring. It wasn't quite the comfort I had become accustomed to at home but I managed to fashion a blanket from some large oak leaves and moulded discarded tissues (filthy humans) together to fashion a pillow. A rather crispy pillow but it did a job.

I thought about the thing in the cage at home, being all warm and cosy, having forced me out of my own pad, making me sleep alone in the dark woods. What an entitled wench.

The following day I continued on my journey, marching along a busy A road. I found it endlessly fascinating to observe humans behind the wheel of their cars. I wondered what makes them become so aggressive just because they are surrounded by a metal cage. They drive too fast, too close to each other, and I even saw some of them using their phone while driving.

I deliberately stepped out in front of one car when I saw the driver was not paying enough attention. That'll learn them, I thought. They swerved to avoid me and called me awful names, none of which I hadn't heard before.

As I got back on the grass verge, I heard something laughing. It was that squirrel again, Bob's mate, from his bestselling novels, *The Satsuma Complex* and *The Hotel Avocado*. I think his name was Carlos.

'Alright,' he said. 'Nice moves back there. I do the same as often as I can. Gets the adrenalin flowing, don't it? Word of warning though, it's a risky business, I've lost many mates under the wheels.'

'You've done good,' he continued. 'I got your first book. Nice read and thanks for the mention. I'm sorry to hear about Dolly.'

I thanked him and then told him I was trying to get back to the dogs' home, which I knew was around here somewhere. He said I was going in the right direction and asked me if I needed anything. I wasn't sure what he could actually offer me but I wished him well all the same and went on my way.

Pretty soon I could hear a familiar howling and barking growing louder in the distance. I was nearly there.

At that moment I nearly turned tail. What the hell was I thinking? Why was I going back to somewhere I had been so desperate to leave?

I'd probably made my point at home. They'd be frantically searching for me and might have even realised it was the French fancy that had made me leave in the first place.

As I'd got this far though, I decided to pop in and say hi to any old mates who might remember me. A little reunion, if you will. Hey, maybe I'd even throw one of my legendary parties to cheer them all up.

As I approached the front door, I noticed the outside of the building looked a little bit different. They'd only gone and put a blue plaque outside to commemorate the time I spent there.

I got up close and saw that it said:

Ted (formerly Billy) lived here 2013–2014

Nice.

I snuck in under a hole by the back fence, removing a rock that had clearly been put there by a previous escapee. Probably Vinnie.

Why are the Danes the only ones to be called 'great'?
I'd like to be called a Great Patterdale.

It was exercise time so they were all out in the yard. At first, I didn't recognise any of my old inmates in the assembled throng. It was packed out in there. It wasn't long before a scuffle broke out and I saw what can only be described as a donkey wade in to sort it out. He put a stop to the nonsense by simply flattening the perpetrators with a swift swipe from one of his paws.

Once things had calmed down a little, I approached the big fella.

'Alright, I'm Ted. I did time here a few years ago.'

'Hi. How come you're back? And wow – what's going on with your teeth?'

'I've not come here for dental advice, thanks. I'm looking for my old cellmate, Pierre. French chap. Big ears. Ring any bells?'

'Oh yeah, I know Pierre. He's not been out of his room in a while. He's in B6.'

'Thanks – nice paws,' I said.

'Nice teeth,' he replied.

I went inside and heard the dismal sound of 'Un-Break My Heart' flowing down the familiar cold corridors. I found Pierre in bed. He'd clearly been listening to the same track over and over again.

He was surprised to see me and looked pretty down in the mouth. He'd put on a load of weight and even his ears had gone a bit floppy.

'Lotta's gone,' he said. 'We'd lived together for nearly a year and I really thought she was the one. But they took her away and they didn't want me to go with them. I've been in bed ever since, bingeing on kibble and scratching my arse on the floor.'

His butt did look pretty sore. Frankly he was in a right state all over. His language had improved. It was now a heady mix of French, Italian and English. He sounded pretty funny but I didn't think now was the best time to bring that up.

I swiftly turned off Toni Braxton and sat next to him. I told him about the foreign object who'd moved into my house and said I'd stay here for a few days and look after him, get him back on all four paws.

I said in no uncertain terms that no one was going to pick him in this mess and we needed to get him sorted out. I made him get out of bed and have a good wash, then I picked off some random fluff poking out of his ears, which made them perk back up almost straightaway. Then I told him to do 20 press-ups. I explained that I would not be taking part in any kind of exercise alongside him as I couldn't be arsed after my long journey to get here.

While he puffed and panted, we caught up on the past few years. He said they'd got a lot stricter in the home and since Vinnie left it was now run by a Great Dane, called Nomad.

Poor old Pierre was in a right stinky state.

Pierre continued, 'There was a riot not so long back. I think they changed the food or something and everyone went mental. They ripped up their beds and smeared the walls with their own poop. The whole place stunk and we were in lockdown for three days.

'I think it was Vera what started it. Looked as sweet as pie but a mouth like a sewer and a terrible temper. She was a genetic mess, a dachshund, collie, German Shepherd mix – she literally didn't know which way was up. Things were a lot simpler when we were all just one pure breed, it's gotten ridiculous now.

'We've had a Chiweenie, Morkie and Bullsky through the doors in the last month alone. They've all got issues because they don't know what they are meant to be or how they are supposed to behave. Vera used to growl at other dogs and then try to herd them up, which was impossible with her tiny legs.'

Chiweenie = chihuahua & mini dachshund
Morkie = Maltese terrier & Yorkshire terrier
Bullsky = pitbull & husky

He had a point. Mongrels are happy accidents and usually turn out to be amazing dogs but recently there's been a frantic craze to mix anything with everything to create so-called designer dogs.

The chap who created the very first litter of labradoodles, an Australian called Wally Conron, once said, 'I opened a Pandora's box and released a Frankenstein's monster.'

I think he's being a bit down on himself. They're not that bad, although there are rather a lot of them around.

It made we wonder what you could breed a Patterdale with to make a daft dog breed. Patterpoo? Patterjack? Patterhuahua? Patman? Pitpatt?

You won't see many Patterdale crossbreeds. That's cos we won't just mate with anyone. We prefer to stick to our own kind.

'How long are you back for?' Pierre asked.

'Couple of days, I guess. Long enough to make them realise they've made a terrible mistake by trying to replace Dolly with some other fruitcake.'

'What exactly is she?' Pierre asked.

'A Brie or something, I think. She's quite pretty but she's massive and she's such a clumsy oaf. Anyway, I don't want to talk about her. Tell me about Vinnie.'

Pierre told me that soon after I left, Vinnie absconded in the dead of night, with my briefcase and a relatively new inmate called Charlie. He explained that Charlie was an incredibly grumpy miniature chihuahua. Apparently, Vinnie stuffed Charlie into my briefcase and they left via the back west perimeter fence.

'Any idea where he was headed?' I asked.

'The gang in the yard reckon he was going to Europe. He'd asked me about how the Channel Tunnel worked,' Pierre replied.

'Did you know?'

'Nope, I didn't exactly get the chance to flick through the promotional leaflets when I was abandoned on it.'

Fair, I thought.

I spent the next few days hanging out at the home, keeping myself well under the radar. As Pierre had cleverly pointed out, I could have been dog-snatched and held for ransom in the wrong pair of hands. When people looked in Pierre's cell, I stayed incredibly still, held my breath, stuck my tongue out and pretended I was his stuffy.

I was really chuffed when, at the end of the week, a lovely French couple chose Pierre to come home with them to the South of France. Wow. Sun, sea, saucisson. I did contemplate asking them to take me as well but I'd miss my fishing trips too much. I was genuinely chuffed for Pierre. He'd been waiting for so long to be 'the one'.

Only another 100 dogs left to go in this home.

Or 199,999,900 still to be adopted worldwide (according to the WHO).

CHAPTER ELEVEN

The Long Way Home

Once Pierre had been snapped up, I thought it was time I returned home and faced the consequences … and that furry frog.

I knew they'd be worried sick about me by now. They'd probably alerted the local media and sent out large search parties. I did like the thought of my face being stuck on numerous lampposts and fences for all to admire, as long as no dog went and peed on them.

I might have even made it onto *The One Show* by now. They'd have any old garbage on there. I once watched the actor Michael Sheen talking about his favourite bus routes.

They'd probably play a video showing all my best bits from *Gone Fishing* with a desperate appeal to find me, probably for a substantial reward. It would rally the entire country in one combined mission. When I eventually returned home, people would be out on the streets applauding and banging their pots and pans in united gratitude.

I took my time getting back. There was no rush and I appreciated they needed time to get together my highlights for the heart-wrenching video.

I played a game of poop bingo along the way to see how many different excretions I could roll in. I ticked off duck, fox, cow and goose – or nature's nougat, as Bob likes to call it. Good name for it; it is rather sticky.

I've discovered recently that foxes are in fact canines – I know, right? That's why us dogs just love to roll in fox poo. They are really one of us, they just don't want to admit it.

I walked in the door and no one batted an eyebrow.

Maybe this was now her house. Maybe they didn't want me anymore.

There was that feeling of déjà vu again. (Really must find out what that means.)

Just when I thought I was all sorted, perhaps life was going to bite me on my fat arse again. I just wished Dolly was here – she'd make everything alright. I did the next best thing – I texted Bob. He was a suitably cuddly substitute.

Ted: Can I come live with you?
Bob: No, I have a cat.
Ted: I like cats.
Bob: No you don't.
Ted: I'll avoid it.
Bob: What's the matter?

Ted: They bought another dog.

Bob: A Patterdale?

Ted: I wish. It's French.

Bob: Cute?

Ted: No. She attacks me 24/7.

Bob: Ted, mate, you gotta stand up for yourself.

Ted: But she has really sharp teeth and she's bloody huge.

Bob: You've got to set ground rules. Like I did with Paul.

Ted: Will you come get me?

Bob: No. We're fishing next week, I'll talk to you about it then. Gotta go, *Real Housewives* is on.

Turns out, the family just thought I'd been away fishing, so they were not at all troubled by my absence. Honestly, what's the point of putting a schedule on the kitchen wall if no one is going to look at it?

If they weren't going to bother with me, I wouldn't bother with them. I decided to go watch *Real Housewives* to find out what Bob found so gripping about it. If you've not seen it, allow me to sum it up for you.

A bunch of very rich, very posh women with nothing better to do argue about really mundane stuff. Repeatedly.

Yep, that's it.

It's like *Loose Women* – if they had more cash to spend.

She looked cute to the untrained eye
but she had clearly left her manners behind,
if she ever had any in the first place.

The French thing was noisily eating its dinner, so I politely waited until she'd finished and then approached her.

I said, 'Listen, whateveryournameis, if we are to live in the same space, you must respect that I am the boss in this house and also please wipe the greasy scraps of meat dangling off your beard before I am prepared to continue this conversation.'

She wiped her mouth with the back of her foot. I was momentarily shocked when I saw the size of her paws. They were now bigger than my whole head.

'My name is Bopo,' she said. 'I'm here to look after you.'

'Bopo? As in Paul's imaginary French clown?'

'Oui. Cute, isn't it? I mean, I could hardly be called Cracker Barrel.' She laughed way too long at her own joke.

Cracker Barrel would have been much more suitable if you ask me – but she didn't.

I stomped my paws on the floor.

'You cannot start muscling in on my fishing gig. If you're gonna stay here, that's clearly a fait accompli ...'

She looked quizzical.

'I mean, there's nothing we can do about that right now but you will never be part of my *Gone Fishing* gang. They're like a second family to me and you are not, and never will be, a part of my family.'

'Je ne comprends pas,' she said, and peed on the rug.

She won't last long here, I thought.

CHAPTER TWELVE

Rules and Regulations

Please can I ask you all a personal question? Why do you insist on changing both your voice and tone when you talk to us?

One minute there you are, chatting perfectly normally, and then you bend down to address us and speak in a manner that can only be described as somewhat childish. It's often incredibly hard to understand and, to be honest, somewhat patronising.

When you issue one of your commands, such as sit/ stay/come, you say it in your normal voice, with an aggressive tinge – and I understand the reasoning behind that. So what's with the baby voice all of a sudden when you are being kind? It makes our skin crawl. And I know I speak for all fellow pets on this point of contention.

It's all over Dog's Net.

I will address your titular musicals at a later date.

And don't play dumb with me, you know you all make up ridiculous songs about our names. Poor old Dolly was often greeted with this: 'Dolly wolly woodle, pot pot noodle, how does your garden grow.' It's a nauseating habit and needs to be stamped out.

The next few months with Bopo tested my patience and pushed me to my absolute limits. She was the closest thing to a bull in a china shop I had ever come across.

She was clumsier than Bob and certainly not as much fun to be with. I was like her personal skittle in her private bowling alley. She knocked me over more times than I wish to recall. She didn't know her own size. She was a very large girl. And I don't mean that in a judgy way.

Dolly was big – but so gentle. Bopo was big and so cumbersome.

Thankfully another fishing trip was coming up, to Blakeney Point in Norfolk. Bo asked if she could pop along and meet the gang but I said there wasn't room for her in any of the vehicles, which was almost true.

I couldn't risk her treading on any of Paul's rods. She'd easily snap them in half if she even brushed past them. Paul tolerates me to a point and I had no intention of pushing it any further with him.

Blakeney Point is on the North Norfolk coast. It's a beautiful national nature reserve and on a good day you can see seals larking about in the waves, if that's your thing.

I remember Bob saying how they look like chubby labradors with their cute, silky black faces but they're a little too slimy for my liking, and I wouldn't trust one as far as I could throw it, even if I could throw it.

There's also a bit of historical beef between Patterdales and seals. Do you remember when a Patterdale had a fight with a seal on the towpath of the River Thames in March 2021? That didn't end well.

Do I really have to remind you to keep your dogs well away from wild animals? I honestly thought that was blindingly obvious.

As it was now summertime, I wondered if I'd need to pack my sunscreen. Dogs are as susceptible to sunburn as humans. It can cause redness, itching and flaky skin, which I have quite enough of anyway. You also need to watch our paws in the sun. They can burn on hot surfaces, like pavements. And please, for the love of dogs, do NOT think about putting us in shoes. It's plain stupid.

I've seen dogs in Crocs, which are just as hideous as the human ones, and anyway, if you are thinking of buying us shoes, then make them designer ones at least.

Talking about humans being plain stupid, can I just take a minute of your time to talk about dogs in cars in the summer? If I hear of one more human leaving their dog in the car when it's warm, for ANY amount of time, please tell them to pay me a visit so we can have a little chat. I'd then wrap them in two (faux) fur coats, shove a woolly balaclava and mittens on, wrap them in a thermal

Now can you see how ridiculous they look?

sleeping bag, seal it up tight and pop them under the grill, on high heat.

Fancy that? Quite.

I don't care where you are 'popping' to or that you 'won't be a second', just listen:

Even on a cooler day (mid teens) the temperature in a closed car can rise to dangerous levels in only minutes. We can expire in 15 minutes. And by expire I don't mean go past our sell-by date, I mean kaput, gone. And leaving windows slightly open is not your get out of jail free card. It won't make enough of a difference.

Got it now?

So much about looking after dogs would appear to be common sense. At least, you think it would be, but time and again I have dogs coming up to me in the park or in the pub with a list of complaints about their owners.

Here are a few, and if you recognise any of these, go make amends with your dog NOW.

'He goes to work from 9–5 and leaves me in the house all alone. I chew everything I can to relieve the boredom and then when he eventually gets back, he shouts at me. I can't win.'

Answer: Take your dog to work if you can or arrange for someone to give them a walk at lunchtime. You shouldn't have a dog if you intend to leave it alone all day. Besides, they'd rather not be with you if that's the case.

'I'm not allowed on the "posh" sofa, only the crappy one in the utility room. How the hell am I supposed to know the difference? I'm not bloody Laurence Llewelyn-Bowen.'

Answer: Either all sofas or no sofas at all, got it? It's called consistency.

'I slide all over the place in the car and don't feel safe at all. Then when I throw up, I get yelled at for making a mess on the seats.'

Answer: It's the law. Rule 57 of the Highway Code says dogs must be suitably restrained in all vehicles. And I don't think that means being polite and quiet. You wear a seatbelt. What makes you think we don't need one?

'I go properly mental when they come back in from a night out but get yelled at for jumping around and making a fuss.'

Answer: Don't go out so much.

Remember this – dogs are part of your world, but you humans are our whole world. Please be considerate – or at the very least, sensible.

CHAPTER THIRTEEN

I Do Like to Be Beside the Seaside

So, off we went to the seaside in Norfolk. I was bang up for this. I do love a run on a beach. The wind in your fur, the sand between your toes. It's the ultimate feeling of freedom.

This turned out to be a shingle beach, which was a tad frustrating as stones are simply not as good on an itchy arse. Sand can act like an excellent loofah, really reaching the bits we can't easily get to, and shingle just isn't up to the job. I had to search out some crispy seaweed instead and used that to relieve my back end.

As I said, it was British summertime. But there was no sun. Completely expected, of course, but nonetheless rather disappointing.

There was, instead, relentless and torrential wind and rain smashing into us at all angles straight from the sea. It was grim and there was no shelter to be had anywhere.

At one point, Bob shoved me up his jumper to try to keep me dry but quite honestly that was an experience

I never want to repeat. I know he was trying to be kind but it was like an Aladdin's cave up there. There were all sorts of sticky bits and bobs clinging to his chest hairs.

They weren't catching any fish on the shoreline either so I sidled up to the crew, picking off the weak ones who were the most drenched, and suggested we round everyone up, call it a day and go to the pub. They were all bang up for that but the director, Rob, said it wouldn't make for a good show. Can't see why not, we'd all have much more fun.

The next couple of hours were some of the trickiest I've experienced on *Gone Fishing*. I can't describe how cold it was. Paul looked like he'd been swimming in his waders. Bob actually had been swimming in his waders as he'd fallen in the sea several times.

I kept well away from the edge of the shore. I knew my little paws would not be able to withstand the pull of the tide. I mean, Bob's quite a solid unit and he was no match for the swell that day, what chance would I have? I know dogs are supposed to be strong swimmers. Paddling with our feet is actually a natural reflex, hence being called the doggy paddle but, although I was blessed with many superb attributes, I was always at the back of the queue when swimming achievements were being shelled out. Shame – I really wanted my Frosties' swimming badge.

Eventually, the cameras stopped working as they were covered in salty sea water and thankfully that meant

One for the road?

we had no choice but to finally pack up. Not a moment too soon.

We escaped to a nearby pub, which is where I famously wedged myself in between the chair and the table. Paul and Bob questioned what on earth I was doing but what they didn't know was that it was all for medical reasons. I'd got whiplash from the rain and wind and had to rest my head somewhere secure before I got a permanent crick in my neck.

To top it all, I came down with a very nasty cold the next day. Yes, dogs can catch colds – look it up if you don't believe me. I had a runny nose, watery eyes, a sore throat and boy did I sneeze a lot.

I didn't tell Bob but I covered his back seat in my nose syrup. I tried to rub it in with my paws, but it was awful sticky and would not shift for love nor money.

Now you know filming isn't all fun and games. There are perfect days when the sun shines, plenty of fish are caught and I have my fill of Spam. Then there are other days where the fish are nowhere to be seen – or more likely Bob loses a couple and then Paul gets all cranky and the weather is grim but we soldier on, for your entertainment. Never forget that. It's a sacrifice WE make for YOU.

You're welcome.

The Troublesome Briard

I'd like to start this chapter with humping – the doggy equivalent of twerking. I don't mean I am actually going to hump something right now. I just want to address the elephant in the room.

I've seen dogs hump anything and everything. Legs: human, table and chair. Cushions, pillows and sofas, mops and brooms. I even saw a Dalmatian hump a car tyre – or try to. It was still attached to the car at the time. Luckily it wasn't moving.

It's just our way of relieving stress or getting rid of excess energy. I s'pose it's the same as you going for a run or having a fag, whichever is your preference.

The key to stopping unnecessary humping from your dogs is to ignore it. I know it's tempting to laugh and, knowing you lot, film it for your socials (#hump) but that kind of attention will only make it worse.

Think of Billy Beefcake down the gym, flexing and showing off his wares in his skimpies. If you take a photo of him, it's only going to encourage him to do it again and again. Dogs, like Mr Billy, will eventually grow out of it.

There was a little bit of downtime before the next shoot so I made a few resolutions.

1. Do not run away
2. Try to lose weight
3. Improve my relationship with Bo

I really couldn't be arsed to run away again but the other two were going to prove trickier to tick off. Food is so darn good and Bo is so darn annoying.

I decided to try to find more about her breed, hoping I'd get a better appreciation of what makes her tick under all that fur. Perhaps if I understood her more, I'd like her more. Her language was slowly improving, and at least I could now understand most of what she said.

This is what I gleaned from my search on the googles:

According to the American Kennel Club, *'The Briard packs so much loyalty, love, and spirit into its ample frame that it's often described as a "heart wrapped in fur."'*

I involuntarily retched.

'The dashing good looks of these muscular French dogs radiate a distinct aura of romance and elegance. Briards are burly and rugged but move with a nimble-footed gait. They possess traits common to many other herders: train-ability, brains, and a protective eye toward their family. These are large, tireless dogs and it is said that just two or three Briards can handle 700 sheep.'

Maybe she wasn't a Briard after all. She certainly didn't have a nimble gait and there was no evidence of any brains in that head of hers either.

Just as a side note, larger dogs have smaller brains relative to their size, which means Yorkshire terriers have the largest brain of any dog, given their size. And big dogs have smaller brains. This makes me pretty smart and Bo pretty thick. Relatively.

Then I read on:

'*During World War I, the Briard was so much a part of the national character that it was named the official dog of the French army, doing sentry duty, finding wounded soldiers, and pulling supply carts. Briards are still used for herding, guarding, police, and military work today.*'

So she has a miliary background, does she ... Then I read something that really blew my mind.

'*Napoleon owned several Briards and took them on many military campaigns.*'

There must be more to this dog than initially meets the eye. I needed to stop seeing her as the enemy and use her more as an ally. With those kind of credentials, she could be just what I needed to get my briefcase back.

I took a pawful of kibble from the treat tin and trotted off to find her. I had intended to use the biscuits to butter her up but unfortunately by the time I found her, I'd eaten them all.

Why couldn't my Briard look as majestic as this one?

I hurried back and grabbed some more, using every ounce of will power to not eat them this time. When I got back, there was one left, which I saw as a small improvement.

She was asleep so I nudged her with my paw. She rolled over and flattened me.

'Sorry, Ted. Didn't see you there,' she muttered.

Standard behaviour. I ate the remaining biscuit.

'Listen, Bo, I know we've got off on the wrong paw but clearly you are staying and I'm not going anywhere either so shall we try to get along?'

'You've never liked me.'

'True. But I am willing to try.'

'It's not my fault I'm not Dolly. She's a hard act to follow.'

'You could start by trying not to knock me over or herd me into a corner every two seconds.'

'I can't help it, I want to protect you.'

'I don't need your protection. I am a fully trained CSO (chief security officer). I protect two A list celebrities and a B list film crew from imminent danger on a regular basis.'

'So you keep saying.' She did a big noisy yawn.

How rude.

Sensing we were getting nowhere, I suggested we attended a local AA meeting – Animals Anonymous – where troubled pets can come together to share their issues with one another in the hope of finding a solution.

CHAPTER FIFTEEN

Turning a Corner

The next day we trudged down to the local church hall. I can honestly say I've never seen a more mixed bag of troubled animals in one place in all my life. Apart from maybe the crew gathering at the hotel breakfast buffet.

A few of the animals instantly recognised me but I felt perfectly safe as I knew whatever happened in that hall would stay in that hall. This was no place for self-ies. Although I did hear a few sniggers along the lines of 'Wonder if he's come to find his briefcase' and 'Where are his celebrity mates now?'

Bo and I sat on a floor mat and were given a warm welcome by the lady in charge, a beautiful red setter called Pink. (I have changed some of the names of the attendees to protect their identity.)

The first to speak were a pair of sibling cats who were adopted together but couldn't stand the very sight of each other. They had come to realise only one could stay at home because the violence was escalating on a weekly basis and was becoming intolerable.

Taking one day at a time ...

Pink suggested the cats gave each other more space and tried counting to ten, then walking away from each other, rather than engaging instantly in a fight. She said they had to realise that if this carried on, one of them would end up homeless again.

They hissed in each other's faces and then both agreed to give this a go as neither wanted to be kicked out.

Next to speak was a greyhound, who I shall call Lady. She was about to be rehomed for the third time, she said, because whenever she was out for a walk, she would race off in large circles and refuse to be put back on her lead.

Pink offered a compromise and suggested she kept it to one circle for now until she'd gained back the trust of her owner.

Next to share her story was a cockapoo, who I'll call Rosie, who said she couldn't help ripping her bed to pieces every night and her owners were now refusing to buy her any more, so she had to sleep on the floor.

Pink suggested perhaps she should rip up their slippers and not her own bed.

My favourite story was from a podgy lab, who I will call Percy, who revealed he kept getting his head stuck in the kitchen bin and it really hurt his ears but he just couldn't stop doing it. The temptation of what lay within the rubbish was too great to resist.

Pink was very considered in her reply. She said to just try, one day at a time, not to put your head in the kitchen bin and to walk away from it. Soon it will be second nature not to go to the bin, but to your own food bowl.

Pink then turned to us, flicked her long red hair out of her eyes and cocked her head on one side. 'Please introduce yourselves,' she said.

'My name's Edward. Bopo here wants to mother and protect me but I can manage perfectly well and I want her to leave me alone.'

Pink thought for a minute and said, 'It's great you have admitted you have a problem with Bopo. That's the first step. Now you need to search for some common interests so that you can try to bond with each other. Is there anything that comes to mind that you both enjoy?'

'Food,' Bo quickly answered.

'Well then, why don't you start by sharing each other's food?'

'We can't. Because he's on a diet,' Bo said, pointedly looking at where my ribs should have been, 'so his biscuits are tasteless and he keeps eating mine.'

Pink tried a different tack. 'Do you both enjoy your walks?'

'Yes,' I replied, 'but she keeps herding me and knocking me to the ground.'

Bo looked suitably sheepish. Pink was firm – but fair – in her response.

'OK, we need to set some boundaries here. Bopo, you need to walk in front of Edward and leave him to catch up in his own good time. Edward, you need to stop taking her food. I think that would be good on several fronts ...' and she pointedly looked at my gut. 'If you ate less, you'd also be able to walk a little faster.'

As we left the hall, when Pink wasn't looking, I helped myself to the biscuits on offer, taking heed of the slogan on the wall: 'progress, not perfection'. (I didn't take *all* the biscuits on the plate.)

On the way home, neither of us said a word. But I did reflect a bit.

And to be fair to her, Bo did walk several paces ahead of me. It was the first time I'd noticed how enormous her backside was.

I knew no one could ever take Dolly's place and I had to admit that it was kinda nice to have company around the house, even if it meant sharing it with a furry space hopper.

I thought on about Bo's breed's military background. I know they helped to find wounded soldiers in the war; I had also read that if a Briard walks past a fallen soldier and doesn't stop to help, it means they are probably not going to make it, and they carry on until they find someone who has a better chance of survival.

I wouldn't want Bo to walk away from me.

CHAPTER SIXTEEN

Vinnie

As I mentioned before, I get a lot of mail these days. I must race to the doormat to get there first otherwise Bo likes to rip it all into tiny shreds and scatter it all over the house, like some kind of demented dormouse.

I got there bright and early this particular morning and there was a large envelope on the floor addressed to me. How very exciting. I wondered if it might be a notification of an OBE or CBE, or maybe I was going to be made a knight. Arise, Sir Edward. That works for me.

Using my teeth, I quickly opened it and carefully read what was inside. It was from Vinnie, the aggressive pitbull I'd left behind at the dogs' home with my precious briefcase. It was brief and to the point.

'I have your briefcase, Edward. Charlie and I brought it over from England at great personal cost. We have opened a commune for stray and unwanted dogs in the South of France. If you can get here with 500 euros, you can have it back.

Postman Patterdale

'P.S.: Si tu dis à quelqu'un où je suis, je jetterai ta mallette dans un fleuve.'

I had no idea what the last menacing sentence meant.

Bo wandered into the hall and sat on my head.

'Please get off me and then can you translate this,' I asked politely.

She apologised, saying she hadn't seen me, and took the letter. After an agonising five minutes she said, 'It says, if you tell anyone where I am, I will throw your briefcase into a river.

'What's this all about?' she asked.

'I have – had – a special briefcase but this Vinnie chap nicked it and took it to France,' I explained.

'Why did he do that?' she asked quite reasonably.

'He found it where I'd left it in the woods, some time ago now, and he kept it as a ransom. How far away is France?' I asked.

'No idea. Where are we now?' she said.

I thought about any of the people I knew who did have brains I could call on, quickly glossing over Paul and Bob.

Lee Mack! Of course, the man who … well, let's just say we had a very memorable time together on Burgh Island when Bob was awash with the shingles.

Lee hosts a very popular quiz show trying to find out who the most intelligent 1% of people in the UK are. He had the brains alright.

I texted him straightaway asking how the heck I could get to France. I got an immediate reply.

Ted, mate. You know we can't talk. What happened on Burgh Island has to stay on Burgh Island. France can't happen. Miss you. LM x

I knew Lee had a family dog of his own who he was very close to and I didn't want to jeopardise that in any way. He clearly thought I was asking him to run away with me to start a new life, which I certainly wasn't. Not this year anyway.

Without a solid plan in place to get my paws back on that briefcase, I decided to sleep on it. I was feeling restless and couldn't switch off so I turned the telly on and watched Noel Fitzpatrick, the self-styled Supervet, mending various shattered bones on various knackered animals.

Don't judge me, I know how much you lot enjoy rubber-necking over *Ambulance* or *999: What's Your Emergency?* It's the same thing. Some have happy endings and some less so, but it's always gripping, if a little gory. I also have to watch it right to the finish to find out what happened to the animals. I know you lot do the same.

Telly people can be quite canny, making sure there's no reason to switch to another side, but you wouldn't do that during *Gone Fishing* now, would you?

Imagine if you missed the ending – you'd never know what happened. Granted, not a lot really happens in our show so you wouldn't miss that much.

It did make me think, however, if we could make *Gone Fishing: The Movie*, an action-packed, watery blockbuster which would break all box office records.

Hugh Jackman could play Paul – they have similar looks and they can both sing beautifully. I'd personally ask Tom Cruise to play Bob. (Yes, I do know him, get over yourselves.) Tom and Bob have a lot in common – sultry good looks, athleticism, style and height. You can imagine Tom pulling off one of Bob's classic falls with total focus and commitment. He does all his own stunts, you know. Bob, I mean, as well as Tom.

Me? I'd get them to make an animatronic model, like they did for Joey, the brave war horse. Imagine the amount of steel they'd need to replicate my teeth, although I'm not sure I'd be happy with a pole inserted up my rear end.

You may think this is a flight of fancy – but just you wait and see, when have I ever been wrong? The movie world are already bidding in huge numbers for *A Pawtobiography* I hear.

I drifted off to sleep thinking about my Oscar acceptance speech.

In the morning, I remembered my mate Pierre. Of course, he was now in France. And *Gone Fishing* were thinking about fishing somewhere abroad for the Christmas special. A plan was beginning to formulate. Slowly. But it was coming.

CHAPTER SEVENTEEN

Going Abroad

The next day I texted Bob.

> Ted: Got any spare pocket meat and can you come over?
> Bob: I'm watching *90 Day Fiancé*. Can it wait?
> Ted: I have Dolly Mixtures.

Bob was a sucker for Dolly Mixtures but he never, ever ate the brown ones, which I fully respect him for.

> Bob: I'll be there within the hour.

And he was – he's such a good boy.

I handed over the mixtures, less the brown ones, and he told me there was pocket meat on the back seat of his car for me and opened the door. Try as I might, I couldn't shift the meaty portions off the seat, even using my bottom teeth like a rake.

'Yeah, sorry,' he said. 'There's something dead sticky on there and I can't seem to get it off. Any ideas what it is? You were in there last.'

Ah crap, my cold.

'I think I remember Paul spilling some of his bait in there. It's probably that,' I explained.

I asked him to come in and he stopped dead in the doorway.

'What the hell is that?' he asked. 'A new carpet?'

'Oh, that's Bo, she lives here now.'

He asked if I was going to bring her fishing and if that was why I wanted the urgent meeting. I reassured him that she was not going to be on the guest list anytime soon.

I didn't really have much time or inclination to make small talk so I cut straight to the grit. I widened my eyes and put my head on one side.

'Please can we go fishing in France?' I asked.

'What fish are there?' he replied.

'How should I know? That's not in my job description.'

'You'll have to ask Paul then. He's the expert fisherman.'

That's news to me. Only jokes. He is a magnificent angler – just as Bob is a magnificent fighter.

'Is there anything else?' Bob asked. 'Only I have to get back to watch *Married at First Sight*.'

After Bob left, I decided to call Paul.

'Alright, Paul. It's Ted.'

'Who?'

'Ted, the dog.'

'Oh yeah, BRILLIANT!'

'Mate, listen, I've heard there is magnificent fishing over in France. Like whoppers and clonkers, literally swimming about all over the shop gagging to be caught. Bob's in – are you?'

Turns out that did the trick and the next thing I knew they were planning a big fishing trip to the Southwest of France.

I didn't tell Bo at first as I knew she'd want to tag along and I was having none of it. Even if she did know the language, I was sure I'd be able to pick it up *tout de suite* as they say.

I needed an AHC apparently to get to Europe. It's an animal health certificate, like a pet passport. No probs, I can get a good mug shot and job's a good 'un.

Then came the bombshell. No teeth were allowed to show in my passport photo. How the hell was I going to overcome that particularly large obstacle?

A dog cannot show its teeth in a passport photo because the photo must show a neutral facial expression with the mouth closed.

I'm not sure my mouth does even close properly.

I spent hours in front of the mirror trying in vain to stretch my bottom lip over my teeth. In the end, I wedged my tongue in the bottom of my mouth, thus pushing my lip up to cover my bottom teeth, but I could only hold it in place for a few seconds at a time.

Fun fact for you, take it to your next pub quiz on me:

A dog's upper lips are called flews. The lower lip is called … the lower lip.

It's impossible to capture my best angle,

maybe I don't even have one.

After many futile attempts, eventually my photo was done. Next stop, the vets. I'd been a few times before, obviously, but since the pandemic it was very tricky to get an appointment.

I didn't care much for the vets – there's never a positive outcome. But to get to France I had to make this personal sacrifice and get checked over.

I will admit, I do like the waiting room at the vets. It's usually a right laugh. I wasn't disappointed this time either. There was a poodle who'd swallowed a bee. I really couldn't keep a straight face looking at her. Her face was so swollen you couldn't see her eyes. She tried to smile at me but her face didn't move a muscle. NGL, reminded me of a few celebs I've encountered.

There was a spaniel shaking like a tree in the corner. I asked him what he was in for. 'I don't really know,' he answered. 'They mentioned something about getting the snip, so I guess it's a quick whisker trim.'

I couldn't bring myself to tell him the truth, so I just said, 'Yeah, it's probably that, mate.'

I turned to where I could smell something quite dreadful coming from under a seat. I don't know exactly what dog it was but he had chronic back-end problems for sure.

'Anal glands,' he whispered, clearly mortified. That can't be fun for man nor beast, I thought.

I waited an age to be seen. Eventually I was dragged reluctantly into the consulting room.

Now, listen up. Dogs have tongues, right? Big tongues, actually. So if you are going to take my temperature, stick the thing under my tongue, like normal people. Since when was putting a probe right up my jacksie authorised?

It was as unpleasant for me as it must have been for the vet, especially as I'd eaten yesterday's leftover curry the night before.

That done, he checked me all over and told me I had to lose weight. No s**t, Sherlock. You went to vet school for seven years to figure that out?

Just when I thought it couldn't get any worse, he got a huge needle out and tapped the end of it, like some kind of deranged professor. 'Rabies,' he said.

Good God, were they giving me rabies? I'd do anything to get my briefcase back but I had to draw the line at rabies. Rabies can kill humans within a week and it makes dogs go proper mental. Rabies literally means rage. What kind of a country was France where you had to have a dose of rabies to get in?

I tried to scramble off the high table. Why on earth do they make them so slippery? It was like a ruddy ice rink up there. But he was fast, I'll give him that, and he grabbed me by the neck. I showed my teeth. Not that I would have done anything bad – I'm a lover, not a biter – but I was trying to warn him to put the needle away and let me go. I was proper fuming.

BANG. OUCH. The deed was done. I now had rabies. Thanks a bunch.

My life flashed before my eyes: the legendary parties in the dogs' home; the joy of arriving at my forever home and meeting Dolly; Bob's endless supply of pocket meat. 'Mind the rod,' I screamed, and passed out.

I didn't actually pass out but it felt like I did. I had a thumping headache and my pads were sweating for Britain, which only made the tabletop more perilous.

This was a nightmare of epic proportions, and I was sure I'd suffer from PTSD (Post-traumatic Stressed Dog) for some time to come.

The monster in the white coat, who was also sweating quite profusely by now, then said, 'You're all good to go to France, little man.'

Talk about pouring insult on injury. So I could go to France now I was laced with rabies? I'd rather not go.

'As you've been vaccinated against rabies, I can issue you your pet passport, my friend.'

This guy was getting way too familiar and why the hell didn't he say that in the first place? I know all about vaccines; we had to have them at the home before we could be put up for adoption.

'Bon voyage,' he chirped as I left. I didn't dignify him with a response.

CHAPTER EIGHTEEN

Parkour – Extreme!

So it looked like a trip to France was on the proverbial cards. I realised I had to get my body into some kind of better shape, or at least a shape.

I took a long hard look in the mirror. Jeepers, my head was half the size of my body. I'd been nicking Bo's big treats whenever I could and I was paying the price.

I'd let myself go. I knew it.

If I didn't do something about it pretty damn quick, they'd be winching me out of the house on a crane before I could get onto the ferry or train or plane or however I was going to get my fat arse over to France.

As far as I'm aware there's no Ozempic on the market for dogs so I had to do this the hard way. I looked up the best exercise for dogs with a fuller figure.

1. Swimming.
Immediately no. I hate having wet paws. I have to manically lick them until they are dry but somehow they always end up even wetter.

2.   Fetch.

I always thought how utterly pointless that is. As soon as you bring the stick/toy/frisbee (delete as applicable) back, they just bloody throw it away again. No, not for me. I'm no fool.

3.   Hiking.

Again, pointless. Climb all the way up a ruddy big mountain/hill/mound/peak (delete as applicable) just to turn round and go all the way back down again.

Nah, none of this was for me.

I nibbled on another biscuit while I thought about what I could do. One biscuit, come on. The horse had long since bolted.

Then I stumbled upon parkour. Or barkour as it's sometimes called on the googles.

Encyclopaedia Britannica defines parkour as:

A physical discipline that involves moving efficiently and fluidly through an environment, by running, jumping, climbing, and overcoming obstacles. The goal of parkour is to navigate through space using only the body, in a way that's quick, smooth, and controlled. Parkour involves: Running, Jumping, Vaulting, Climbing & Rolling.

Gripped – I read on:

It's not just about doing tricks or stunts – it's about efficiency, fluidity, and smooth movement. Parkour is also a philosophy, emphasizing freedom of movement, personal expression, and overcoming both physical and mental challenges.

Sign me up. Hold on, can dogs take part?

While it's not the same as human parkour, many dogs can perform impressive feats of agility, strength, and coordination that resemble parkour-style moves. Some dogs, especially high-energy or athletic breeds, are trained to navigate various obstacles like jumping over walls, climbing ramps, or weaving through bars.

Right, I'm in. I am a high-energy, athletic breed. This is me to a tee.

I went into the woods to limber up. I started slowly, carefully navigating my way over very small sticks. It wasn't as easy as it looked.

Luckily I was well used to tucking and rolling. I'd perfected it after months of constant body blows from Bo.

After seven minutes I was knackered. This sport was not for the fainthearted – clearly why it suited me so well.

I practised every other day, gradually building up my strength. When I was feeling more confident about my growing ability, I went down to the local skate park where there were bigger concrete structures to navigate.

There I met a right feisty little terrier called Rock. He was built like a brick poop house and his moves were out of this world. I watched as he threw himself at a wall, scaled it and then jumped back down in the blink of an eye. It was an incredible sight.

He told me he was trained by the best, a border collie called Ninja. He'd seen Ninja perform at the Goodwoof Festival (yes, honestly) in Sussex and was hooked from that moment.

'It's not only great for your body, it's good for your mind too,' Rock explained, seeing me wide-eyed at his slick moves.

'Let me show you the kong vault.'

He ran towards a concrete block, used his front paws to vault over it and then tucked his back legs under and carried on running as he landed.

Yep, I thought, I can nail that.

I ran towards the block, leapt up – all good so far – but I forgot about the last vault and skidded across the block on my teeth (creating some good sparks) before flopping on the floor and skidding several yards on my front.

Luckily, because of my ample frame, my belly took the brunt, so it was like landing on a pillow and although I was winded, no lasting harm was done.

Rock loved it, particularly the added firework effects. He said I showed great potential at the sport.

From then on, we'd meet in the park every Tuesday night and he'd help me perfect my technique. After

There's more to this parkour lark than
meets the eye – or the teeth.

training, we'd go to the local pub and greedily hoover up chips and crisps from the floor.

Rock and I grew quite close. He was pretty rough and ready but who was I to judge the backgrounds of others? I was no Crufts champion.

Crufts … the canine equivalent of Miss World perhaps? Over 200 breeds compete for Best In Show every year, but wrap your head around this if you can, Patterdales are not allowed to enter the main competition. Probs 'cos we'd wipe the floor with every other entrant. The only trophy won by one of my tribe was in the aptly named Perfectly Imperfect Category at Crufts in 2016, by a little fella called Sab – a good win for him as he was permanently scarred after being used for badger baiting. See, true beauty always lies within.

Crufts was started in 1886 by a man called Charles Cruft, who was a dog biscuit manufacturer. It was originally a show for terriers only and went downhill from there, obviously.

I asked Rock about his past. He told me he used to belong to a lovely family but one day he got lost while they were on holiday and out for a long walk in the Lake District.

He said, 'It was such a beautiful place, acres and acres of open spaces. We'd go for wonderful, never-ending walks every day …'

He stopped and his big brown eyes filled with tears.

'One walk did turn out to be never-ending. I lost sight of them around Derwent Water and the more I looked, the more I realised I was just going round in circles. I panicked and just ran and ran. I did hear their voices at one point, and I ran in that direction as fast as I could but then I just didn't hear them anymore.

'I don't know how long I'd been missing as I lost all track of time. Eventually, maybe after three or four days, I found my way back to our little holiday cottage. The adrenalin was coursing through my paws. Finally, I thought, I've made it. I knocked on the door with the biggest smile on my face but to my horror a different family were standing there, staring back at me. Mine had gone.

'I've been homeless ever since. That was a good few years back now. I was only young. I loved my family so much I just didn't want to live with another one and I've heard horror stories about dog wardens and dog homes so I just kept myself under the radar.'

'That sucks,' I said.

He replied that he'd got used to it now but he hadn't given up hope of one day finding his family. Meanwhile, he said, 'the parkour helps keep my mind off it and I can travel all over the place finding new ways to challenge myself. And maybe one day I'll be reunited with them.'

CHAPTER NINETEEN

The Big Plan

That night, when I got back home, I thought a lot about Rock, the poor little sod.

I knew he wasn't alone. According to Petlog, over 10,000 dogs go missing *each year* in the UK. And in case you're thinking that it's somehow our fault, let me inform you, humans lose around 8 million mobile phones each year according to mobiles.co.uk. Just goes to prove how irresponsible you lot can be.

I mean, 8 million? If you can't keep hold of your precious phones, it's little wonder you can't keep your eyes on us. You obviously need to be reminded of the golden rules of dog ownership yet again.

1. Put a tag on our collars – NOT with our name but with YOUR phone number.
2. Microchip us.
3. Use a harness, not a collar, so we can't slip out and run off, particularly when we are young.
4. TRAIN us in recall. Sounds obvious, this one, but make sure we will come back to you when you call

us. Remember we can get easily distracted if we get a strong scent and we don't have the benefit of Google Maps about our person.

5. Keep an eye on us during walks. Put your phone away (if you haven't already lost it), stop gossiping with your mates and make sure you know whereabouts we are.

And one final thing: please, please don't yell at us when we do come back. We live in the moment and will only think you're cross because we have returned, which will in turn mean we take off again!

No excuses, people. It's your responsibility. We can't microchip ourselves, can we?

I have put a few contacts at the end of my book to help if you do lose us, you're welcome. I shan't tell you again.

Right – back to ME.

I only had a few weeks left to prepare for the big trip to France. I hadn't really lost much weight, probably no surprise considering the amount of chips we scoffed after training.

It gets harder to lose the timber as you get older, even for dogs, as our metabolism slows down and, for me at least, my desire for treats only grows.

I met up with Bob and Paul to discuss the trip, which was to be our Christmas special. I asked Bob if he'd been working out and before he could reply, I said, 'Didn't think so.' It was just our joke.

Meeting with the big cheeses – and biscuits.

Paul looked as fit as ever and I noticed he declined the biscuits on offer, while Bob and I tore through them as if our lives depended on it.

We were meeting to discuss our ideas for the trip. For clarification, I had none, save to find Vinnie and get my briefcase back. They blathered on about the fish and their tactics for sometime, while I had a snooze.

I woke up when they started talking about the Annual Awards Ceremony. I tried to work out if I had a shot at Employee of the Year. I'd had an exceptional year, let's face it. I'd been superb throughout the last 12 months, I think we'd all agree.

I gathered we were going to stay in a chateau, which sounded promising. Paul was thrilled to hear it was on the site of a vineyard and so was I. Do you know what hangs out in French vineyards? A lot of mice and voles. They're from the same family, I think, but voles are stockier with smaller ears and are a LOT harder to catch. Game on!

Turns out, Paul, Bob and the crew were going to fly to France but I wasn't allowed. I was fuming. Did they expect me to bloody walk all the way there?

No, I was to go on the Eurotunnel, they explained. This was a train that ran under the English Channel. I remember Pierre talking about it. I wasn't keen. How the hell does a train run underwater? How wet would my paws get?

Didn't sound like I had much choice in the matter. I'd get there a couple of days later than them, which worried me about the bedroom-picking situation. I'd have to get extra crafty.

When Paul left the meeting, I tapped Bob with my paw and said, 'A word, please.'

I explained I'd found out that Vinnie was in France with my briefcase and asked if I'd be allowed to take a leave of absence during the shoot to try to find him. I didn't mind forgoing a day or two's pay.

Bob reminded me that I didn't get paid anyway. He said it would be fine as long as I didn't miss the Awards Ceremony (my hopes were getting higher) and as long as I would be safe.

'Yes, about that,' I said. 'I think I may have to bring bulky Bo along as she speaks the language. Is there room for her?'

He said it was up to me but she was not allowed to share a room with either him or Paul.

Understood. Whilst I didn't relish the prospect of bunking up with her, I thought she could turn out to be pretty useful.

What I didn't mention to Bob was that I intended to bring Rock along as well. I thought he'd enjoy the adventure and he was a strong, streetwise lad (Rock, not Bob).

PART DEUX
FRANCE

CHAPTER UN

The Briefcase

I am very well travelled around the UK thanks to the amazing places we go fishing. We have explored the length and breadth of the British Isles – and of course the lads have been to Ireland too.

Just thinking about the places we've been makes me feel so privileged. Dorset, Norfolk, Scotland, Surrey, Wales, Devon, Yorkshire, Derbyshire, the Peak District, Nottinghamshire, Essex, Shropshire and of course old Father Thames, to name but 15.

Taylor Swift, eat your heart out. *That* is a tour.

I am usually the last person to know where we are going. That kind of knowledge is beyond my pay grade – which is not hard as I'm on a zero-hours contract. I don't do this for the money – which is just as well. What would I do with money anyway? There's nothing I really need or want. Can you imagine me with a Rolex or a Hublot Big Bang on my paw? Having said that, a chunky gold chain round my ruff could suit me, don't you think?

I do dabble in that popular big house draw. An upgrade to my lodgings will always be welcome even if the fast-car prize would be a tad useless. I've never won, anyway.

Now, talking about trying your luck, let me touch on scams. We are not immune to those either.

I was nearly caught out recently by a romance fraud. A beautiful labradoodle, somewhat ridiculously called Doodle, was sending me saucy pics and sweet messages and I admit, I was immediately suckered right in. She said she'd been following my career since the first time she saw me on the telly, that I was clearly the real star of the show, I had the most magnificent teeth she'd ever seen and she had posters of me on the wall of her crate. It was all very flattering.

Then she said she knew where my briefcase was and if I could just send her £500 in Pets At Home vouchers, she'd take me straight to it.

I smelt a rat straightaway. I'm very good at smelling rats. It's in our breed DNA.

I asked her why she wanted the coupons and she said she needed to see an emergency vet because her paw had dropped off unexpectedly overnight. She sent me a picture of her paw – except it didn't match her collar and cuffs.

I blocked her. Just remember, if it sounds ridiculous, it usually is.

Now I had to pack for France. Where do I start?

I could already tell it was going to be like travelling with a Tasmanian Devil.

I had my animal health certificate, a good dose of rabies and some insect repellent. Which might come in handy on Bo. I also packed a deck of cards for the journey, my tuxedo and a small hairbrush.

Before we left, I felt nervous but excited. Bo was beside herself and bouncing over everyone and everything, like a bloody hairy tornado. Rock was just grateful to be invited.

I managed to get hold of Pierre. He sounded out of breath and explained he had some mates round for a pool party.

'What's it like over there?' I asked him.

'Food's good, weather's great, we are allowed to eat out in restaurants – but word of warning, do NOT ask for your steak to be well done. They hate that.'

I explained I was coming over with the *Gone Fishing* gang so steaks were not going to be on the menu.

Pierre continued, 'It's a great place. You'll love it. They are all about holidays over here. They work to live as opposed to grinding every gear on the rat wheel to stay afloat.'

That'll suit the lads, I thought. They don't like to work too hard.

'I need to find Vinnie – and Charlie, if he made it in one piece after being trafficked across the Channel in my briefcase.'

Pierre told me the word *en France* was that the pair of them were hiding out in the mountains somewhere in the South, where they'd opened a commune for unwanted dogs. They were totally off grid and free range and it was heavily protected by packs of vicious guard dogs who were looking for any excuse for a fight.

Sounds inviting, I thought. Wonder what their star rating was on Tripadvisor.

Pierre told me to be very careful, that the letter could have been a trap set by Vinnie. He asked if I had back-up and if Bob and Paul were coming with me. I said it was far too dangerous for celebrities of their calibre but that I was taking the canine equivalent of Little and Large with me.

'Oh well, at least you'll have a good laugh then,' he said.

CHAPTER DEUX

Gearing Up

I gathered the troops and checked their luggage. Bo wanted to take her eyelash curlers and I couldn't be bothered to argue. Rock was taking nothing. I guess he didn't really own anything of his own. We all bundled into the car for the first part of the journey.

The next few hours were hell on a stick. It was so squashed in the back of the car. Bo's arse took up about 90% of the seats, leaving a measly 20% for me and Rock. He ended up on the floor but I was determined to hold on to my place, however uncomfortable I was.

We couldn't agree on the music either. I wanted to listen to some hip hop, Bo pleaded for yacht rock and Rock was intent on playing high-energy disco. In the end we sat in silence.

We did have snacks but after a while the car stank of rancid meat. I think it was mostly from Bo's backside.

Finally we approached miles of lanes and bollards and lorries and kiosks and queues and screaming kids and barking dogs. It was like driving into Lidl on a Saturday during a half-price sale.

Then we were loaded onto the waiting carriage.

We were sitting in a car on a train about to go underwater. It couldn't have felt more twisted. My mind – and my heart – were racing.

Bo stared gormlessly out of the window and Rock sweetly held my paw.

It took days and days to cross the Channel. I'd been told it was about 35 minutes but I don't know who the hell made that up. I did know the bit under the water was 23 miles long and that didn't help matters one little bit.

I couldn't really wrap my head around the fact we were over 300 feet below sea level. It felt wrong and dangerous. This wasn't even a submarine and I'd seen *The Hunt for Red October*, where things went really tits up.

What if someone wanted to open a window? Mind you, the view was crap; it was horribly dark when you were under the water. Safe to say I didn't really enjoy much of it.

I gather when they built the Tunnel, there was a team digging from France and one from the UK at the same time and when they met in 1990, they were 14 inches out of alignment. Sloppy really, innit? Wouldn't have happened on my watch.

When we arrived there was a tedious wait while they checked through all my paperwork once again. There were quite a few other dogs waiting in the queue, so we passed the time with a sniffathon.

I wondered why they were all making this perilous journey. I know a lot of British people go over the Channel to stock up on cheap French booze. Maybe the French equivalent of Bonios were half price in France?

After everything had been stamped time and time again in what appeared to be an utterly pointless exercise, we were let out to visit the restrooms before continuing our onward journey.

I was busting to go. Being surrounded by so much water had been torture.

The pet exercise area was by the side of an old garage and a fast-food restaurant – you know, the one that sells a Royale with cheese. The glamour of it all was not lost on any of us. I was rapidly losing enthusiasm for this trip. Was it really going to be worth all this hassle?

We piled back in the car for about three weeks (they told me it was two days) and continued through France. The roads were quieter than the UK but as we were driving on the right-hand side, cars coming the other way seemed dangerously close to us and I couldn't bear to look out of the window.

Luckily, this time Bo sat up front – yes, in a seat belt, so put your pens down – leaving plenty of room for me and Rock to sprawl out in the back, although we made sure never to touch each other's fur – it would give us both the ick.

Hoping the long trip to France will be worth it.

It was dark by the time we made it to the delightful Château Camp del Saltre in Cahors, where the rest of the crew were already hanging out. Paul and Bob were rather surprised to see me. I think they thought I'd be stopped at the border or deported back to England before I set a paw in France. O ye of little faith, I thought, not really knowing what it meant.

The crew were clearly delighted to see me, although somewhat surprised to meet Bo and rather confused when I introduced Rock. I heard someone mutter, 'I thought this was *Gone Fishing*, not *Gone Dogging*.' Now there's an idea.

I explained that Bo was French and could come in handy, although she should be kept at arm's length, particularly near anything delicate.

Bob took me to one side and said, 'I knew you were bringing the woolly mammoth but what's with this other little fella?'

I explained that I had found him and he was homeless. I put my head at an acute angle and begged, 'Please can we keep him?'

Bob said as long as he didn't eat as much as me and was fully house trained he could stay for the time being. I humped Bob's leg lightly to express my gratitude.

I told Bo and Rock to sit and stay while I went upstairs to nab the best room left. I wanted a comfy double bed and a good view of the vineyards.

I explained to Bo that she couldn't sleep on the bed as it was highly illegal in France, but I had special permission. I told her she would have to sleep on the floor and Rock said he'd be happier sleeping outside anyway. I think Bo's rear emissions during the long drive had put him off sleeping in the same room as her. I wasn't entirely without blame on that front either.

After I unpacked, I went downstairs to join the others. To my horror, Bo was flat on her back, paws in the air, legs akimbo, with the crew all fussing over her while Rock looked on, mouth open.

I said I needed an urgent word with Bo and took her to one side. In no uncertain terms I told her to pull herself together and display a bit of decorum, as opposed to displaying her wares. I said this was a professional job and she had to act accordingly. There are strict procedures and guidelines in place for inappropriate behaviour in the workplace and I felt I had no choice but to give her an immediate formal warning. She went off with her tail between her legs and I took my rightful place, on the lap of one of the cameramen.

It was Toby, if you must know. He's always had a soft spot for me, apart from when I had a wee on his waders – while he was wearing them. I'd never done it before and shall never do it again. I'm not sure what came over me. I think he's forgiven me. It was simply a moment of madness. I'm sure we've all had a few of those, haven't we? I mean, when you gotta go, you gotta go.

Now I'd had my first proper taste of France. I'll be honest, I wasn't that impressed. Same old crew, same old faces. Just a different country. I don't know what I had expected. I thought maybe they would have surprised me with my own personal assistant for this trip. I did, after all, have quite a lot on my plate, not least wrangling Bo and Rock, finding Vinnie and my briefcase, and of course my personal performance had to be top notch for a Christmas special.

I can guess what you're thinking right now. 'Ted, you just hang around a riverbank, eating pocket meat and bait, rolling about in whatever you can find before irritating Paul and Bob.'

That takes work, my friends, proper graft. I have to make sure I am in the right shot at the right time as well as the wrong shot at the right time. I can't bark willy nilly all over their lines, not that I bark and not that they have lines, but you know what I mean. Do you realise the willpower it takes not to run over to the fish they catch and give it a good lick before they put it back? Or the skill involved in treading exactly on the right spot, in the dead centre of Paul's fishing rod, over and over again.

Yes, I make it all look easy. But that's the prowess of a truly gifted actor.

CHAPTER TROIS

To the River

None of us stayed up late that night. There was plenty of work to be done in the morning and I wanted to make sure I looked my very best for this 'special' Christmas show.

Breakfast involved a crashant or something, which was a little dry and covered me in flaky shards of pastry that stuck fast to my fur. Also, to my immense pleasure, there was a wide selection of meats and cheeses on offer. Breakfast meat? Yes please. And if that wasn't enough, it was all presented in a buffet style. I made a mental note to get there extra early the next morning to get my fill.

After we'd all stuffed our faces, we piled into Bob's hire car to get to the River Lot.

As soon as I got in, Bob lobbed me out again and told me to have a good shake to loosen the pastry crumbs off my body. He wasn't this fussy in his own car, I thought. Just cos this was a hire car, he'd changed his tune and come over all 'la di dah'.

Bob's driving in the UK is sometimes questionable, and average at best, but put him in a new car on the wrong side of the road and it's a whole new ball game. I could see Paul's knuckles turn white as he gripped the seat and I watched his feet desperately trying to press the brake pedals, even though they weren't on his side of the car. It was a little like being in a tumble dryer – not that I have, but you know what I mean.

It didn't take long before Bob drove over a bollard or a kerb or something and scraped all along the bottom of the car, making a dreadful crunching sound. (If Enterprise are reading this, it didn't really happen like that. I just made that bit up.)

Paul got out and walked the rest of the way to the river. I decided to brave it out because I couldn't be bothered to walk. The relief was palpable as we all piled out, shaken and stirred, by the river.

The drama of the journey soon melted away as we settled down to fish on the banks of the River Lot. It was very beautiful, calm and serene. We were surrounded by stunningly tall cliffs and it felt like we were all alone in our own little private world. It was like a scene from *Jurassic Park*. Have you seen that? No, nor me.

That's one of the many special treats on *Gone Fishing*. It often feels like we are miles away from anything and anyone. Even for a dog, to just sit still, take in your surroundings and breathe in the fresh air was an incredible tonic. To be present – not to think about what to chase and when to chase it – or what to roll on – but to just 'be'.

In our happy place.

Rock went off to find somewhere to parkour and Bo stayed by the car. I think she was still a little bit shocked by Bob's, what I'd loosely call, driving.

My inner calm was broken by those two muppets laughing their socks off. Bob was asking Paul to reel off his best-known characters and catchphrases and it was a comedy masterclass. Dogs can't really change their bark tones so I'm always very amused when Paul or Bob play their comedy cards.

I particularly love Bob's waiter when he pretends not to be Bob although I don't fully understand how he does it and why Paul doesn't recognise him at first. I just can't work it out and I think it confuses Paul too.

If you are questioning if dogs have a sense of humour, firstly why did you buy this book and secondly, I can assure you we certainly do. Whilst we don't exactly laugh like you lot, we make a sound known as a play pant. It's a fast heavy breathing noise, which is our way of showing we are excited and having fun. If you've never heard your dog make that sound – take a good look at yourself before blaming us.

Paul and Bob were nattering on the riverbank about the year they'd just had, talking about how time flies as you get older and how every Christmas seems to come round quicker and quicker the older you get.

Last time we'd been out fishing, I didn't really get what they were on about and tended to switch off when they discussed serious stuff like ageing but now I was getting older, I was beginning to understand what they meant.

They discuss their own mortality a lot, but I hadn't really thought about it until Dolly died. I wondered how long I had left and shuddered at the very thought of not being around anymore. I'm sure it's just as hard for you to imagine a world without me too.

There was no denying I had slowed down a bit. I no longer had the will to pointlessly chase squirrels and my legs were a little stiff. I put that down to all the parkour training but when I last looked in the mirror, I was shocked to see how grey I'd become.

It looked like I had a bloody pair of glasses on. I'd also lost a couple of teeth but luckily right at the back of my mouth, not my powerful front jobs. They were still standing at least.

I realise none of us know how long we have left. Be cool if we did though, wouldn't it? If I knew I only had 24 hours, I'd go back to Chesil Beach, where Paul, Bob and I enjoyed a delicious picnic of mackerel on the beach as the sun set.

What about you – what would you do?

Don't worry about answering that. I'm not really bothered and besides I won't be able to hear you.

I guess all we can do is truly live in the present and appreciate the simple little things in life, like unexpected extra pocket meat and a warm bed or whatever it is that floats your particular vessel.

'*The future depends on what you do today*' – Mahatma Gandhi said that. Never met him, but he sounds pretty switched on.

I could spend hours listening to Bob and Paul just chat nonsense to each other. Which is just as well in this job. They have the ease of people who have known each other for a long time, because they have. They've been friends for like 30 years or something. Thirty years! Us dogs get to know people for a maximum of about 14 or 15 years if we're lucky. It's not very long, is it? Go give your dog a squeeze from me right now.

I am now 13. I tried to work out how many weeks, days, hours and minutes I might have left. If I lived another 2 years, that's 730 days. I was beginning to feel short-changed.

My musings were shattered by an almighty commotion up by a nearby lake. Deep in thought, I hadn't noticed that Bob and Paul had moved on to a new place to fish.

I told Bo to come and watch the magic happen. Together we ran to where it was all kicking off. Paul and Bob were involved in a tug of war with a ginormous fish. A carp, I later gathered. It was too big for the net and too far down the riverbank for them to catch. The whole scene was an absolute sh*t show. Two of the crew had fallen into the river and the sound man, Sam, was hanging on by a thread – or a tree branch, to be more specific.

Bob was obviously flat out on his arse by this point. He never stood a chance.

I swear to God the carp rolled his eyes at me.

Eventually the big fella was on dry land (the fish, not Bob) and there was much celebration and self-congratulation, before, as per usual, the fish was gently put back into the water.

Bo was confused. Doesn't take much, as well you know by now. She didn't understand why we would all spend so much time, energy and emotion catching a fish only to put it back in again.

'Bo,' I said, 'you have much to learn about fishing.'

Job done, we all headed back to our accommodation. Paul drove this time, much to the obvious relief of everyone on board. I even kept my eyes open most of the way back.

CHAPTER QUATRE

Back to the Chateau

Back at the chateau, Paul and Bob were treated to an exquisite meal cooked by a wonderful French chef called Patricia. She spent hours preparing it and the smell that wafted through the entire chateau was like nothing I had smelt before.

I mean, I've had some good whiffs of Bob's bankside cuisine, but this was in a different league. Do you remember the tripe? I swear I can still smell that in my sleep.

I hovered under the kitchen table as Paul and Bob literally lapped up the dinner. I was praying for some scraps or crumbs to come my way but they ate every little piece and with each mouthful proclaimed how unbelievably tasty it was.

They were like a pair of greedy gannets. I drooled so much on the floor it looked like I'd wet myself.

I sidled up to Patricia, gave a quiet little sigh and opened my eyes as wide as they would go. Then I said in my very best French:

'Ça fait plusieurs jours que je n'ai pas mangé. Puis-je lécher la casserole s'il vous plaît?'

She smelt as good as her cuisine, let me tell you,
maybe a little less meaty.

Which means, in a nutshell, 'I haven't eaten for days. Please can I lick the pan?'

She made sure Paul and Bob were not watching and quietly put the dish on the floor for me. It was liquid gold and I'll never forget it.

My whiskers were a tad greasy afterwards so I slipped out of the kitchen and wiped my mouth along the length of the sofa, first one way and then back the other, leaving a telltale tide mark which I'm sure will fade in time.

Before anyone had the chance to notice my messy misdemeanour, I distracted them with a surprise Christmas present I'd arranged for Paul and Bob. It was a personal message from the England football player Phil Foden. I'd met Phil a while before down at my local five-a-side footy club. I didn't play football because my legs are a tad too stumpy but I went along as often as I could to support my mates and get in on the snack action at halftime.

The team was called Liverpoodle FC and they were close to the top of the K9 FL. Our secret weapon was a beagle called Geoff. He never took his eye – or his paw – off the ball and he was a top scorer – even against our rivals Leads United, who had a very athletic border collie in goal.

We always drew quite a big crowd and we were firm favourites amongst the England team lads. They'd often pop by on their way back from their training to support us.

I had no idea so many of our Premier League football players were such big dog fans. Raheem Sterling has a rottweiler, Jack Grealish a Belgian Malinois, Kyle Walker a Dobermann and just when I thought I had it all figured out with tough dogs matching tough guys, I found out Jordan Pickford has a cavapoo and Declan Rice a cockapoo. I correctly guessed what kind of dog reliable, cuddly Harry Kane would have – a labrador.

Funny how we pick dogs to suit our characters, probably without even knowing it. I mean, look how similar I am to my on-screen owner Bob. Bit grubby, rotund, sometimes athletic, cuddly, incredibly funny and with a magnetic personality.

It's not just football players who get dogs that mirror themselves, it would appear. Simon Cowell has a small and fierce Yorkshire terrier. Holly Willoughby has a pretty and soppy golden retriever. Lewis Hamilton has a bulldog. Although I gather the tall radio lad Vernon Kay owns a chihuahua. What's that about?

So along comes Phil Foden with his French bulldog called Carabao – after the Manchester City cup win of the same name, I gather. Just as well they didn't win the FA Cup that year – imagine calling sweet FA in the park, FFS.

Turns out Phil is a big fan of fishing. Carp is his thing, so I asked him to record a festive message for Paul and Bob. When I delivered it during the Christmas special, the lads, being big footy fans themselves, were well chuffed. He wished them a very merry Christmas and promised to try to join them fishing one day. Watch this space. Good karma points don't earn themselves, now do they?

CHAPTER CINQ

Mission Impossible

Stuffed full of good karma, I decided it was the right time to go fetch my briefcase.

The only information I had, from Pierre, was that Vinnie had opened a large commune for unwanted dogs somewhere in the South of France. France is more than twice the size of the United Kingdom, so this was not gonna be easy. We knew his commune was somewhere in mountains but there again there are seven mountain ranges in France.

Rock smartly asked who had the original letter from Vinnie. I did, in my suitcase. It had a postmark on it. Of course it bloody did. He didn't hand deliver it, did he? The postmark on the envelope said Toulon and there was a logo at the top of the letter:

The Pit Stop – a Canine Commune.

Quite smart, I thought, for Vinnie.

So we knew what and whereabouts. It was the how that was the current sticking point.

At breakfast, after I'd steered clear of the crumbly crashunt and gone for the altogether smoother brioche, loaded with saucisson, I asked Bob if he could give the three of us a lift to Toulon. He said he couldn't for two reasons: they had to film more fishing and my breath stank.

I thought that was a little unnecessary extra detail but the saucisson was pretty strong to be fair and it was starting to repeat.

He said if we did go by ourselves, to make sure we were back in time for the Annual Awards Ceremony. It was sounding obvious to me that I'd clinched Employee of the Year and that's why he wanted to make sure I would be there. It would only be the second time I'd won this most prestigious of awards, and I began to compose the speech in my mind, making a mental note of who I should thank:

1. Me

Before all the glitz and celebrations could start though, I had to get that briefcase back.

I began to imagine what it would be like to be crowned Employee of the Year with my briefcase by my side. It was the stuff dreams were made of. The crew all cheering, Paul and Bob in floods of tears ... an expectant crowd waiting to greet me outside. The media clambering to get the perfect shot of me. With my newly acquired parkour skills, I might even try a bit of crowd-surfing.

First, we needed to get to Toulon. It was 11 hours by bus or 7 hours by train. This was going to be a marathon, not a sprint. We decided to take the high-speed train, the TGV – or in French parlance, Train à Grande Vitesse. I liked the sound of that.

Rock, Bo and I had a logistics meeting. Of course, I'd done this sort of thing before on many night manoeuvres and surveillance operations and Rock was well used to travelling far and wide, but Bo wasn't exactly stealthy and, whilst I will admit she was very pretty, she was also incredibly thick. I decided to put her in charge of interpreting. Rock's job was travel co-ordinator and I was in overall control of the entire operation.

We only had 48 hours to get into Toulon, find Vinnie, get the briefcase and get back to Cahors. It was going to be tight.

I'd been in tighter spots but not in the company of the equivalent of Mr Blobby and Usain Bolt.

We went through our checklist of what to take:

Bolt cutters. Snacks. Euros.

Rock took the bolt cutters, Bo the euros and I had the snacks.

The next morning we set off very early and took the bus to the train station. Most dogs go free on public transport in France but because of her size, Bo had to pay, which highly amused me and Rock. It wasn't quite so funny when we realised she used our kitty of euros to pay.

'Not my fault I'm plus size,' she muttered. I guess she did have her own seat, whereas Rock and I were on the floor.

Bo really was such a lummox. Travelling with her was like trying to take a large sack of potatoes from A to B, without the assistance of a sack.

The French have a wonderful phrase for someone like Bo: 'con comme une valise sans poignée'. Which is like saying they are as useful as a suitcase without a handle, which I thought was pretty apt.

Her interpreting did come in handy, particularly at the station when we had to change trains and get the right one to Toulon with minutes to spare.

However, we ended up in Marseille.

On the train ride back to Toulon, we made use of the free wifi and tried to narrow down the search for Vinnie's Pit Stop. I tried to think like Vinnie. He liked woods, he liked freedom and he held grudges.

What could possibly go wrong?

CHAPTER SIX

The Pit Stop

Toulon is a city on the French Riviera, also known as the Côte d'Azur. It's home to 70% of the French naval fleet and there is a national naval museum by the harbour, so if all else failed, I knew I could while away a few happy hours with the local sailors in the port.

Rock pointed out that there was a cable car in Toulon which took people to the summit of Mont Faron (which is a mountain, Bo helpfully added) and at the top there was a wooded area of several hectares. It was a strong start and the only lead we had, so we grasped it.

Once in Toulon, we took the Téléphérique du Mont Faron. I've never been in a cable car before and I was utterly terrified. I tried not to show it but my legs shook like jelly and I couldn't look out of the window. It was a horrendous two-hour journey which took seven long minutes.

Rock loved it – he wasn't afraid of anything – and Bo, once we'd humped her into it, asked if we were there yet every two seconds.

At the top it was really rather beautiful. We could see the whole town of Toulon and the harbour underneath us but there was no time for sight-seeing and we headed off into the woods.

By now it was getting dark and it was eerily quiet. The tourists had all hopped on the last cable car back down the mountain and there was nobody around. They had, of course, left plenty of rubbish behind, which was very thoughtful.

We decided to trek on for a couple of hours before making camp for the night. I was used to traversing through woods, as was Rock. Bo moaned every ten minutes about pine needles and bugs getting trapped in her paws. At first I nibbled them out for her, but after about 20 minutes I'd had a gutful of French bugs and they were starting to repeat on me.

We found a clearing by a picnic table. Handily it had half-eaten jambon baguettes trampled into the ground underneath it. That was supper sorted.

The sun was setting and it was getting a little chilly so all three us of huddled under the picnic table, sweeping aside the assorted crap people had discarded. Rock and I cuddled into Bo for warmth. No, I'm not going soft on her. I was cold, OK?

It was anything but a quiet night. I could hear endless cries and howls of big cats, wolves and monkeys and they seemed awfully close. I didn't know if it was a dream or reality but I didn't like it one bit.

Dog ears act like radars and our hearing is ten times more accurate than yours. Remember that next time you curse us under your breath – we can hear you loud and clear! When we don't hear you, it's because we choose not to.

As the sun rose, I crept out from under the table. Bo and Rock were still out of it. I had a good look around in the daylight and then realised we'd camped very close to a ruddy zoo.

The faded sign said 'Zoo Fauverie Du Mont Faron'. I decided to check it out. It was a pretty sad-looking place. I don't think zoos are an attractive proposition to begin with and this did nothing to promote the brand. The animals looked lonely and bored. I did contemplate letting them out with our bolt cutters but I didn't fancy being a Happy Meal for a jaguar and made a mental note to mention this place to Vinnie.

Heading back, I woke the others up, and once we had all finished our morning ablutions, we set off again.

Pardon me for a little aside here, if you will. Let's be honest, you don't have a choice, unless you want to skip the next paragraph. Up to you.

In the UK, each dog produces about 340 grams of waste per day, which adds up to around 3,000 tonnes between us.

That's a lot of crap. To put it into context, it's about thirty times as heavy as a blue whale. Three thousand tonnes of poo, droppings, waste, stools, packages or business a day. Call it what you will – that's a heck of a lot.

Think about that next time you pretend not to notice your dog going in the park, or worse, on the street. PICK. IT. UP. Make sure the bag is biodegradable; the scent is your personal choice. I favour lavender.

I guess we walked on a couple of miles before we saw a large compound looming in the distance, partly covered in trees and brush. The familiar sound of dogs barking rang in our ears. We knew we were close. My heart started pounding and my mouth went so dry my teeth stuck to my flews.

As we carefully approached, we could see several big French mastiffs patrolling the area, inside tall wire fences. They looked pretty ugly and mean to boot. Not that I would have booted any of them.

Rock scaled a fence to get a better look at what we were up against. After his third ascent, he landed back with eyes wide. He told us there were about 40 dogs in there of different sizes and shapes and they all looked pretty rough. Each corner was covered by at least one of Vinnie's guards.

We sat in silence for a while, working out our next move.

'Where's Bo?' I asked Rock. We both looked but couldn't see her anywhere.

Then we heard a commotion in the distance by the far fence. Bo was nose to nose with one of the guards, wagging her tail. What the hell was she doing now?

We lay low until she came back. When she returned, she had a sparkle in her eye and a swing in her step.

'What's going on?' I asked her.

'I used every ounce of my native French charm, batted my long eyelashes and flirted like my life – and yours – depended on it. I have agreed to go on a date with one of the guards, a fairly pleasant young chap called Marcel, down by the harbour tomorrow evening.'

She continued, 'In return he told me about a small hole in the northwest fence. Or was it the southwest? Either way it's over there.' She pointed to the far corner of the compound. 'I'll go back to Marcel now and chat about our dinner plans. You two go find that hole.'

Rock and I looked at each other and then back at Bo, agreeing that was quite a bold move on her part. I told Rock to scale the fence while I dug under where Bo had pointed.

We could see Bo was now surrounded by four or five beefy mastiffs but she was holding her own pretty well.

Rock and I crept along the ground on our bellies, which was somewhat tricky for me as my gut kept getting stuck in the mud. In the end Rock went behind me and shoved me along, leaving a deep trench in our wake.

Rather her than me.

We saw a half-collapsed shed in the distance and could make out '**Pit Stop**' cleverly spelt out with bark and twigs. This was clearly Vinnie's HQ.

I told Rock to stand guard outside. I took a big deep breath and knocked on the door.

'Vincent, it's Edward.'

I thought that was a more businesslike way to start.

'Come,' barked a familiar voice.

And there I was, face to face with Vinnie and his little sidekick Charlie the chihuahua.

'Sit. Stay,' Vinnie barked.

I guess those words are ingrained in us dogs and I instantly did as I was told.

For a while we just stared at each other. Then Charlie limped over to me and sniffed me thoroughly, which was an unpleasant experience for us both.

'What's with the leg?' I asked.

'I got my paw trapped in your bloody briefcase,' he snarled back. 'That thing should come with a health warning.'

I was going to mention it was designed to be used for important papers and not as a transportation device, but it was clearly a little late to point that out.

Once he was satisfied I had no weapons stashed about my person, he hobbled back to sit next to Vinnie.

Vinnie then piped up:

'So you got my letter then? Did you bring the cash?'

I didn't answer him straightaway. I could see my briefcase and I'm sure it was glowing.

'Is that what I think it is?' I asked him.

Vinnie, sitting astride my briefcase, nodded slowly.

His dirty butt was resting on my most treasured possession.

In our defence, dogs, of course, don't have access to toilet paper and we have pretty furry arses. I mean, there is bound to be some collateral damage, isn't there? Bear with us, and the odd swipe with a wet wipe every now and again would be welcomed.

For us, not you, I get that.

I asked Vinnie what he was doing over here and he told me he'd opened the Pit Stop over a year ago. He continued:

'I escaped from the dogs' home and decided to leave the UK. I was sick of the grey weather day in, day out and I just couldn't see any of the benefits of Brexit, so thought I'd try my luck in Europe. I'd heard Pierre talking about Le Shuttle so I grabbed Charlie, who also wanted out, and we made for Folkestone.'

'Why did you stuff him in my briefcase?'

'He didn't have a passport.'

'Did you?'

'No, but I knew no one would dare question me. Anyway, we made it to France, with a little bit of unfortunate damage to Charlie's paw, which he has not stopped banging on about since – talk about ungrateful.'

What a sight to behold.

'Pit-bully,' Charlie muttered in his strong Mexican accent.

Ignoring the little fella, Vinnie continued:

'We settled in quickly to life over here. What I wasn't expecting was the sheer amount of stray and abandoned dogs I saw. I mean, they were everywhere. It seems over here you are either pampered to within an inch of your life or chucked out on the streets without a backward glance.

'I found out France is known as the "European champion" for pet abandonment. I asked one of the chaps I met on the streets what it was all about and what he told me really shocked me. He said every year over 100,000 pets are abandoned. The French love their summer holidays, and the schools shut for two months, so rather than be faffed travelling with their pets, they just discard them. Turns out the shelters get full by the start of the summer.

'This poor chap I met had been left with just a bucket of water outside the town hall while his owners buggered off to Saint-Tropez to top up their tans. With the shelters full, you know what's next ...'

And Vinnie crossed his neck with his paw.

We all shuddered in unison.

'Not saying all French owners are like this, but it seems there's plenty who are. I decided I'd done enough damage in my life and maybe it was time to help my comrades out here on the streets. So I opened this commune. I don't turn any dogs away and it's heavily guarded because the authorities want to shut us down and send us all to the knacker's yard.

'I was running out of food and money and the only asset I had was your briefcase – so I wrote to you. I knew you had a good heart and I knew you wanted your brief-case back so, as they say over here, voilà! You give me the money, and I give you your handbag.'

'Briefcase.'

'Whatever.'

'Slight issue, Vinnie,' I said. 'We spent most of our savings getting here and, er, on biscuits, so I only have five euros left.'

I swallowed hard.

There was a long silence.

Eventually Vinnie sighed and shook his head vigorously, wobbling his sizeable chops from side to side, sending out a spray of warm gob all over Charlie.

I tried to suppress a laugh but holding my breath only led to an illicit tommy squeaker escaping from my back-side. Rock coughed outside to cover me. Good lad.

'What was that?' Vinnie growled.

'That's my mate Rock. He's homeless as well.'

Rock, hearing his name, burst in.

'Are you checking in?' Vinnie asked.

'No, thank you. I'm only visiting,' Rock answered.

There was another long silence before Rock said:

'If you need money, why don't I put on a parkour display for the tourists in the harbour? We'll put out poo bags for them to chuck their euros in and give you the cash we raise.'

'What the heck is parkfloor?' Vinnie asked.

And with that Rocky leapt up, bounced off the walls onto the table and up the side of the shed, finishing with a forward roll and a mighty flourish.

'That, my friend, is parkour. Extreme,' he said.

Vinnie was suitably impressed with this impromptu display. We all shook paws (apart from Charlie as he'd fall over) and the deal was sealed.

Vinnie slowly pushed my briefcase towards me. I quickly grabbed it and tucked it under my paws, being careful to only touch the very edges.

We rushed out of there.

Crap – I'd forgotten all about Bo, on a speed date with a slobbery guard, poor girl.

I need not have worried. Bo was playing a blinder, rolling about on the floor, all legs and fur, and the mastiffs who had gathered to watch were transfixed.

Rock and I grabbed her on our way out and got the hell out of Dodge.

CHAPTER SEPT

The Show Must Go On

That evening in the town square, Rock played an absolute blinder. He busted out all his big moves, including a wall flip and a double kong, ending with a cat grab. It was impressive stuff.

The crowd went wild. We raised 172 euros, no doubt helped by Bo fluttering her long eyelashes and being generally rather cute. French people are suckers for Briards and she was a good-looking blonde one, I have to admit.

We passed the cash to Vinnie, who was watching the show alongside his pack of loyal mastiffs, although it was obvious they were more interested in Bo than the show. They were stood in a pool of their own drool. Least I hope it was drool.

Before we left, I told Vinnie about the zoo and how sorry I felt for the animals that were kept there in far from ideal conditions, and he promised to investigate. I knew he'd keep his word, so we wished him well and set off for the station.

Everyone lapped up the performance.

We were in a proper hurry to get back. I was probably about to be crowned Employee of the Year and it was high time I returned to my day job.

On the way, I asked Bo what had gone down with Marcel.

She said, 'It all moved rather quickly. He asked me to come and live with him in the commune. He thought I'd make a wonderful asset to the management team and I would be very welcome here.'

My ears pricked up, metaphorically. They can't stand up by themselves without the assistance of wind.

If she stayed here in France, I'd have the whole house to myself again and I'd no longer have to live like Inspector Clouseau in the *Pink Panther* movies, dodging the furry equivalent of Cato Fong round every corner.

'So what did you say?' I asked, not really knowing what I wanted the answer to be.

She replied, 'I said I'd need to think about it. I mean, it would be nice to live somewhere I am wanted, where I have a purpose and am perhaps even loved.'

Ouch. How is it that the female of the species always know how to get you right where it hurts? It's like their superpower.

We stood and stared at each other without saying another word. Bo turned to look towards the commune in the distance and then back at me. She did this several times.

Eventually, I sighed and said, 'Come on, let's go home.'

With that she leapt on top of me, rendering me in the full splat position.

'That's your problem, Bo,' I said. 'You just don't know your own size.'

'Am I big then? she asked.

'Look,' I said, 'I'm sorry I was harsh on you. I just …'

'You don't have to explain,' she said. 'I get it. I'm not Dolly.'

'No, and you never will be, but that's no reason why we can't rub along together.'

I tried to pat her on the back, only I couldn't reach that far.

As we approached the town centre, Rock suddenly stopped dead in his tracks. He was staring at the entrance to the train station, eyes and mouth wide open.

'I think that's my family,' he slowly said.

I could see two big humans and two smaller ones, all wearily dragging their cases out of the concourse.

Rock's tail wagged so hard I thought he might take off.

'Go on then,' I said. 'Go back to them. Now's your chance, quick!'

Then we both spotted the same thing at the same time. They had a puppy on a lead. It looked a little like Rock.

Rock didn't move a muscle and we watched silently as the family got into a waiting cab.

Eventually he said, 'I think it's too late. I'm a street dog now, I s'pose. I'm not sure how I'd fit back into a family routine and it wouldn't be easy sharing my life with a new puppy.'

I couldn't argue with that.

'It's been a blast meeting you two. Hold on, where's Bo?'

Bo had her head stuck in the bottom of a vending machine on the station platform.

'Say goodbye to her for me. She's a good sort really. Good luck with the rest of your jaunt and bring that trophy home!'

And with that he was gone, sliding down the staircase railings and slipping into the night.

Bo eventually wriggled her head out of the machine and was triumphantly holding a big packet of macarons as we got on the train. We both slept pretty much all the way back and finally returned to the chateau at about 2am.

Everyone was already asleep. Bo and I went to our room and I let her lie next to me, which I instantly regretted as she took over the whole mattress. I had to cling on to the edge like a mountain goat all night.

The Annual Awards Ceremony

Bob and Paul were pleased to see me back safe and sound – when they eventually noticed I was indeed back safe and sound.

I asked what they'd been up to and they told me they'd been tasting the wine from the vineyard. Paul is pretty knowledgeable about wine, while Bob prefers his beer. I like water. But, even though I like it, I don't find it necessary to drink gallons of it like you lot do.

There is only one species in the world that can't get drunk. An Oriental hornet. But then again, they probably don't need to get hammered. No one's gonna invite them to their summer garden party.

I wanted to find out more about what the big deal with wine was. There were a few bottles with some dregs left over round the back of the kitchen, so I stuck my tongue in and had a quick lick. It was like putting my tongue down a drain. We have 1,700 tastebuds – none of which would appear to be stimulated by wine.

I also feel it is my duty to inform you that we can instantly tell when you are three sheets to the wind, trollied, sloshed, battered, plastered, blotto, tanked, blitzed or legless, despite your protestations that you've just had the one.

We can tell through your body language, smell and behaviour. And the fact you come home much later than you promised. Not that we judge you at all.

After breakfast, it was a right old frenzy of activity in the chateau as we all got prepped for the Annual Awards Ceremony, perhaps the most significant date in our fishy calendars.

I got out my finest tuxedo – I only have the one but it is mighty fine. It still fitted me, which was both a surprise and a relief.

Bo said she'd stay behind. She appreciated that it was my special night and she wasn't going to give me any shade. She made sure I looked smart and sent me on my way, saying she was looking forward to seeing the trophy later.

We arrived in a blacked-out, chauffeur-driven car. I sat in between Paul and Bob in the back. There was no small talk on the way as we were all quite nervous and it was a tight fit.

I'm not sure what either of them were wearing. They'd been to a thrift shop in France while I was away and looked like a pair of clowns in second-hand suits that were far too big for them. I wondered if it was supposed to be a fancy dress evening and I'd missed the invitation.

The awards were held in a very posh hotel, so I wiped my paws thoroughly before going in and made a mental note not to scoot along the obviously antique rugs lining the long hallways.

The first award was a new one, for Mucky Old Man, which was a surprise to both me and Bob, although not entirely gratuitous. I knew this was going to be a close contest and would probably come down to the wire. The immensely talented Richard Ayoade was to announce the winner. I met him at a special book night in London last year and I will admit, he's a bit of a hero of mine.

The nominations were played out and I grew ever more confident. They picked the bits of me peeing too close to Bob's sardine supper, rolling in muck several times, scooting down riverbanks and eating the bark off a tree, which is full of nutrients, actually.

Bob's best mucky bits included dropping assorted ingredients on the ground and trying to hide it from Paul, dripping egg all over his coat and then licking it off, and of course his stand-out moment of belching profusely after downing a bottle of lemonade in one go.

Paul said it was going to be a photo finish. Then, barely managing to contain his obvious excitement, Richard announced the winner.

Bob.

Disappointing but ultimately the right call.

With only one award remaining, the smart money had to be on me clinching EOTY.

They played out our best moments from the last series: the lads catching clonkers and of course me wedging my head in the table at the bar. Surely that had nailed it. It was such a terrific move on my part.

Bob had the envelope. My mouth was dry. My paws were sweating. I looked across at both Paul and Bob – they looked just as nervous as me. This was a BIG deal.

Bob slowly opened the envelope. The entire crew collectively held their breath.

'The Employee of the Year is … Paul.'

He was delighted. I was crushed.

Maybe there was another award? Top Dog? Most Improved Player? Goal of the Month? Album of the Year? I didn't care, I just wanted to be recognised for something.

While Paul celebrated with Bob, I slipped outside, pointedly marking my territory as I left on one of the posh rugs.

I sat outside overlooking the incredible views of the Lot Valley, with the River Lot gently flowing through it. Nature was beautifully oblivious to the dramatic scenes that had just unfolded inside.

I gave myself a good shake. You probably know when a dog has a strong shake it relieves all their stress, and it did help.

I realised I was so lucky to be here. What did an award really mean? It wasn't like I could eat it. I s'pose I could have buried it but either way, it wasn't mine.

Just as I was pondering the outcome of the evening, a French mime artist called Benoît, who had entertained Paul earlier, popped up out of nowhere. He could see I was pensive and sat down next to me. His beautifully painted face did give me a bit of a start but then he slowly pulled an invisible thread from his heart with his white gloves and offered it to me with a soft smile. He pressed his palms together and bowed slowly, before walking quietly away.

I had absolutely no clue what he was doing or what it was supposed to mean, but it was fairly pleasant to watch.

Paul and Bob came out of the hotel shortly afterwards and scooped me up in their arms. Not going to lie, it was a bit of a struggle as I'm a bit of a lump these days, but we had a giant group hug. Bob whispered, 'You'll always be the grubbiest' and Paul added, 'We all know you're the real star of the show, Ted.'

He didn't say those exact words but I'm pretty sure that's what he meant.

The strange man in the striped shirt.

CHAPTER NEUF

Party Time

Back at the chateau, I went straight up to my room. The crew were throwing a party as it was the end of the shoot but I didn't really feel like joining them straightaway. They'd be up half the night anyway and I'd catch up with them all later.

As I opened our bedroom door, Bo instantly saw my paws were empty but said nothing, which was a smart decision of hers under the circumstances.

Frankly, if I wasn't going to be recognised in any category at next year's awards, I'd quit and join *Extreme Fishing* with the hunky Robson Green. As long as he promised to never sing.

There was no point dwelling any further on what might have been. It was time to reunite with my briefcase. This was going to be the real trophy of the trip.

'Bo, pass me my briefcase, please,' I said.

She just looked blank. I mean, she always did look pretty vacant but this time all the colour appeared to drain out of her fur.

'I don't have it,' she said.

Nor did I.

A dreadful silence hung thick in the air. Neither of us knew quite what to say next.

Then Bo whispered quietly, 'I think I *might* have left it by the vending machine. I remember putting it down when I went in for the snacks and then we had to race for the train ... I remember holding the macarons, but only the macarons.'

The silence returned, only even thicker this time.

I hadn't checked if we had it on the train either.

I weighed up my racing emotions: anger, disappointment, disbelief, frustration, sadness, resignation.

We'd come all this way to a foreign land, I had been forcibly injected with rabies and for what?

No briefcase, no award and no tan either.

This was not the outcome I had expected.

I couldn't go back to the train station as we were due to leave the next morning and I certainly didn't want to stay in France any longer.

Bo said she wanted to join the party downstairs but I really wasn't in the mood to boogie. Anyway, if Bo was on the dance floor, I'd doubtless get crushed.

I did what any self-respecting little dog who was in a massive sulk would do. I went to bed and relentlessly licked my paws.

It was hard to sleep with all the noise downstairs. It sounded like they were having a lot of fun, which I thought was entirely unreasonable. I decided I wouldn't talk to any of them the next day.

In the morning, Bob sat next to me at breakfast and gently took my paw. I noticed his hand was almost as hairy as mine.

He said Bo had told him last night about what happened at the station and that she was really sorry.

I nearly answered him but remembered in the nick of time I wasn't supposed to be speaking to anyone.

Bob continued, 'We all make mistakes, Ted. I shouldn't have done my own dentistry, but we eventually learn to live with the consequences.'

I wasn't entirely sure what he meant – I'd always thought his teeth were rather striking. Anyway, I made my excuses and politely left the table.

I kept up my vow of silence on the long train journey back and played cards with the crew, steadfastly giving Bo the cold shoulder, which I'm not sure she even noticed.

It did feel good to be back home again, in my own bed with my own special smells. I took the opportunity to carefully reflect on the trip.

Never mind your hand – gimme your breakfast, mate.

CHAPTER DIX

I've Started so I'll Finish

I was so lucky to be a part of the Christmas special, on an all-expenses-paid trip to the South of France with the people who meant the most to me. And Bo.

I had completed my first voyage out of the UK. I had travelled underwater. I had driven on the wrong side of the road. I faced off an enormous French carp. I found and lost my briefcase.

I tasted a Royale without cheese. Actually without even the bun. Or sauce. Or gherkins. Or tomato. OK, so I had a bite of a French beef patty. And I licked a macaroon.

I also foiled an attempted armed bank robbery and led hundreds of passengers to safety when the French metro's electric system spectacularly failed mid-tunnel, for which I was awarded the prestigious Legion d'honneur for exceptional services to France.

Did I not mention that before? Oh sorry, there's no time to get into that now, we're almost out of pages. I'll have to write another book.

The best fishing buddies in the world.

Safely back at home, I began to consider: Did the briefcase really mean that much to me or are all possessions ultimately meaningless compared to love and forgiveness?

Nah, no way. I loved that briefcase. It was all I really had in the world.

Then again, didn't I have so much more than an old, stained and soggy satchel?

I slowly began to realise I did.

I had a companion who was willing to risk her own well-being to make me happy. I mean, Bo nearly went all the way, quite literally, to help me out in Toulon.

I also had two old (in both senses of the word) fishing buddies who brought me unadulterated joy and would never let anyone harm a whisker on my face.

Sometimes when we lose something precious, we fear it will change us forever and stand in the way of any future happiness. But maybe the opposite is true. Loss doesn't have to be the end. It can mark the beginning of a new chapter.

Remember earlier on in this gripping tale, when I said one of the hardest things about losing Dolly was that the world kept on turning and nothing changed around me? I felt I'd lost something that would never be replaced. But now I realise it doesn't need to be replaced. It needs to be cherished for what it was.

Life often lobs things at us that can make us feel like the sun is setting and we are going to be plunged into darkness. But one thing is guaranteed. The sun will ALWAYS rise again.

Even if big old Bo is blocking the light, eventually she, or the sun, will move and you will feel warmth again.

Enjoy every day the sun shines on you, dear friends.

Since we can't know how much time we have, the best thing we can do is live like every day matters – because it bloody well does.

Postscript

Bo and I are now good pals. She will never take Dolly's place and she doesn't want to. She did replace my little toy sheep that she ate when she was a puppy. I shouldn't really have been surprised that she replaced it with a fluffy goat. Her heart was in the right place. She's still a massive, clumsy oaf but then nobody's perfect, are they? Well …

I put Dolly's collar back on top of her ashes. I didn't feel the need to sleep with it anymore. It was time to return it to her.

I heard often from Rock. He was adopted by the National French Barkour Team and was touring all over the world doing his thing.

Vinnie's commune is still going strong and his mastiffs made it very clear to the guards at the zoo that they needed to up their game. If you pay that place a visit, let me know, won't you, so I can report back to Vinnie.

Following Rock's amazing parkour performance, which raised awareness as well as cash for the Pit Stop, the public had started donating food and beds to Vinnie on a regular basis.

And me, what's next for me? More fishing, of course, with the best pals anyone could wish for. Maybe I'll even catch a fish myself one day.

Sometimes real friendship takes time to grow.

Appendix

Those of you who contacted me on Instagram (@ted_gonefishing) after reading my first book, please refrain from calling me cute, a darling, a little poppet, a real sweetie or, worst of all, 'pawgeous'.

Let me ask you, would you call Vinnie Jones or Jason Statham those names?

Exactly. Think about that next time you get in touch, please.

* * *

Want to know what Bob's head tasted of?

Pepperoni with a little hint of lime.

* * *

Millions of dogs are beneficiaries in their human's wills – just putting it out there in case you have read to the very end, PAUL & BOB. I will leave you Bo to share, of course. FOC.

ESSENTIAL FRENCH FOR DOGS

Avez-vous de la viande de poche?
Do you have any pocket meat?

Attention à la canne à pêche!
Mind the fishing rod!

Est-ce que vous l'avez dans une plus grande taille?
Do you have it in a larger size?

Excusez-moi, votre pied est sur ma patte.
Excuse me, you're standing on my paw.

Faisons une grande fête.
Let's have a big party.

Ne vous noyez pas dans un verre d'eau.
Don't drown in a glass of water.

RESCUE CENTRE REPORT

This is the original paperwork pinned to the outside of my kennel in the rescue home.

It's a bit like a school report. I hope you noted the words 'bright' and 'lively'; I probably would not have been adopted if it had said 'He's a bit of a pain in the arse and needs a lot of work but give him a shot.'

DIANA BRIMBLECOMBE ANIMAL RESCUE CENTRE

ANIMAL'S NAME   **BILLY**

ID: 7012

BREED   PATTERDALE X

DESCRIPTION   BLACK

Age   ? 7 MTHS

Sex   Male   **NEUTERED**   YES

Vaccine Status: PARTLY   **MICROCHIPPED**   YES

FURTHER DETAILS

    GOOD WITH CHILDREN: Over 12s

    GOOD WITH OTHER DOGS: Yes

    GOOD WITH CATS: No

Cute little Billy was given as a Christmas present, then dumped into rescue in the New Year when they decided that dog ownership was too much like hard work!! All relationships worth having involve some work, don't they?! Fortunately for Billy, instead of having to go into rescue kennels at this formative stage of his life, he instead was taken into a foster home, so he has learned to be a really good boy, and more importantly, has learned that people will love him, and that he can love them back.

He has also learned to live happily with other dogs, and will tolerate cats, but will probably be too much for all but the most resolute of felines.

Billy is a bright, lively pup who will need an owner who enjoys terrier temperament, and who has an active lifestyle.

Like any dog of his age, training classes will be essential if he is to remain the lovely little chap he is now, and he will need company most of the time.

A DOG'S TAIL IN DETAIL

I've had a tail job. Not by choice you understand.

I don't understand why you lot like to change your bodies by reducing or plumping or tightening or lifting different parts: why not be happy in the skin you're in? Ever seen a dog with a bum lift or a tummy tuck? I could do with both, granted.

My tail was 'docked' or more accurately put, chopped off, so I have a stump or what I like to call a 'nubbin'. It still works, just not very well. Docking is now banned in UK unless you have a very specific reason for wanting a tail-less dog.

Bo has a huge tail, which she puts to frequent use, removing glasses from tables or vases from the side, much like a wrecking ball.

Hers has a majestic and destructive swish – mine has an almost imperceptible twitch.

A dog's tail is an extension of our spines and its primary use is for communication. We even have 'wag bias', which means we can move it to the left or the right, as we choose; right being happy and left being less so. Mine just goes up and down. It's like a broken grabber machine at the fair. But then again, I'm always happy so I don't really need extra indicators.

Our tails are rather like your hair, they can be curly, straight, short or long.

The main difference is they don't thin out or disappear completely as we get older.

And, much as you might admire an older gentleman with a thick thatch, we too can suffer from tail envy. A chihuahua's tail is only 5cm long whereas a Great Dane's tail can reach lengths of over 45cm. You don't want to share a bath with them in the groomers, let me tell you.

And consider this, if you joined together all the dog tails in the world they would wrap round the earth 5.6 times.

You do the maths, you know by now I can't.

There are 900 million dogs worldwide with an average tail length of 25cm; and the earth's circumference is 40,000km.

WHAT TO DO IF YOU LOSE YOUR DOG

1. Don't panic. 93% of lost dogs are reunited, most within the first 12 hours of going missing.
2. Check in and around your home and garden. The little sod has probably found his or her way home.
3. Call and verify their microchip contact.
4. Work out your search radius, starting from where they went missing.
5. Report them missing to local dog wardens, animals shelters and the police.
6. Use social media and get posters printed – try to use a nice mug shot.
7. Most importantly, remember when you get them back, don't shout at them for running off. They won't understand why you are angry and not delighted. Give them a big hug and don't let them out of your sight again.

Here are a couple of organisations that can also help.
https://www.doglost.co.uk
https://www.rspca.org.uk

RECIPE

Like Bob and Paul, I know I must try to eat more healthily.

Bob's guilty pleasure, as we know, are cheesy Wotsits and bacony Frazzles. I do love a crispy snack myself, so give this one a whirl. It's a recipe for crispy cheesy chews, which I like to call Pocket Chumps.

1. Slice some sweet potatoes into thin rounds and sprinkle both sides with a little olive oil.
2. Bake them for three hours at 120 degrees.
3. Take them out of the oven (carefully) and while they are still warm, sprinkle each one with a little bit of low-fat cheese.
4. Allow them to cool before scoffing.

And remember, please snack responsibly.

TOP TEN DOG NAMES IN UK

As of 2025, these are the most popular dog names in the UK:

1. Luna
2. Bella
3. Teddy
4. Lola
5. Milo
6. Willow
7. Poppy
8. Ruby
9. Buddy
10. Bailey

These rankings are based on data compiled by Pets at Home's Pets Club, which has over 8 million members.

I fully expect to claim the number one spot next year and appreciate that is up to you. I'm counting on you.

FAMOUS LAST WORDS

I will leave the final words in this book to my two bosses, Bob and Paul.

BOB

'When I think of Ted, I think of biscuits, Spam, ammunition, goose droppings and old water because that's what he smells of. When I am with Ted, I don't think of those things at all because he's the perfect pal.'

PAUL

'Ted turned to me recently with that mournful yet devoted expression you see in man's best friend and said, "You two muppets would be nothing without me. I should knock you both spark out." Then off he went, leaving behind a fetid, pungent pong, reminiscent of Bob.'

ACKNOWLEDGEMENTS

TED would like to lick Bob, Paul and all the *Gone Fishing* crew: Toby, Barney, Andy, Sam, Matt, Natalie and Johnny. Also, John for finding the best fishing river-banks to fish in and for me to roll in and Mr Doug for the classy edits. He'd also like to thank the lovely *Gone Fishing* viewers for making him the star of the show!

LISA would like to thank:

Bob and Paul, Stephanie, Rob, Louise, Andre and Georgia, as well as Patrick for keeping the show on the road.

Lorna, Michelle, Shelise and Lucy at Penguin Random House.

Gordon at Curtis Brown and Camilla at STV, Chiggy and Claire at PBJ and Jaquie at Curtis Brown.

David Clark for his creative influence, Jonathan Clark and my own very special boys, Dan, Jon-Joe and Archie.

Becki at Surrey Canine Corner for the play dates.

Final thanks to Ted and Bo for allowing me to be their voice and giving me the pleasure of writing this book.

Fabranese Cupcake 'Dolly'

2008–2021

'A dog's love is eternal; their memory everlasting.'